THE CND STORY

THE
CND
STORY

The first 25 years of CND in the words of the people involved Edited by John Minnion and Philip Bolsover

MARCH FROM
LONDON
TO
ALDERMASTON

...TION
DEFENCE M...
18 FEB. 1961

...IZEN...
...RVIVAL
BAG

CND
...EWARD

**Allison & Busby
London**

First published 1983 by
Allison and Busby Limited
6a Noel Street, London W1V 3RB

British Library Cataloguing in Publication Data:
The CND story
  1. Campaign for Nuclear Disarmament – History
  I. Minnion, John   II. Bolsover, Philip
  327.1'74   JX1974.73

  ISBN 0-85031-486-0
  ISBN 0-85031-487-9 Pbk

Set in 10/11 pt. Bembo by
Derek Doyle & Associates, Mold, Clwyd
and printed in Great Britain by
Richard Clay, (The Chaucer Press) Limited, Bungay, Suffolk

CONTENTS

A section of the huge crowd, estimated at about 250,000 in Hyde Park, 6 June 1982. (*Photo:* David & Katie Urry.)

PREFACE

CND membership has grown more than tenfold in the last three years; the largest demonstrations in the Campaign's history were held during 1981 and 1982, the attendance of both estimated at about a quarter of a million people; and there are more CND groups across the country than ever before. Moreover, with the aid of strong allies, the Campaign has for the first time forced a government to retreat on an important national issue – the Hard Rock national civil-defence exercise, cancelled by the Home Secretary on 14 July 1982.

This book offers a wide range of impressions of the movement's first twenty-five years, and a variety of views on issues that have been and are important for the Campaign. Forty people, all of whom have been active in CND, contribute short articles which are grouped into eight chapters (the first four chronological, the last four thematic). As a framework, the Introduction offers a brief historical summary of CND since its origins in the 1950s.

In our view, CND's strength lies in its diversity. For this reason we have encouraged contributors to present their own views on the issues raised, and to draw on their personal experience of the movement. This is, therefore, a collection of individual views from within the Campaign, and in no sense an "official history".

The contributors include people from many different strands of the movement, though obviously we do not claim that this is an objective cross-section of CND supporters – whatever that might be! About half are, or have been, full-time workers for CND or related organisations, and these include all who have served as general secretary of the Campaign except for the late Peggy Duff, to whom the book is dedicated. (Peggy was, in fact, planning to produce a book similar to this for Allison and Busby before she died in 1981.) Five of the nine people who have chaired CND are also included. Most of the contributors, but by no means all, were active in the Campaign during its earliest years; every one of them remains a committed supporter today and has expressed the wish that all royalties from this book should go to the Campaign.

Our very sincere thanks go to all the contributors who generously made time to meet a very tight deadline, and who often helped in many other ways as well as writing their own articles. In addition to them we would like to thank warmly our long-suffering families and many other people whose help, advice and encouragement made this book possible. They include Stan Banks, Anny Brackx, Philip Braithwaite, Sheila Cooper, Godfrey Featherstone, Olive Gibbs, Elizabeth Goffe, Henry Grant, Dave Hinton, Adrian Howe,

Judy Hubbard, Susan Lamb, Tony McCarthy, Pauline & David Schiff, Tony Schramm, Theresa Stewart, Maurice Tildesley, and Diane Nason, whose efficient help with the typing was indispensable. Many thanks, as well, to the staff at Allison & Busby for their swift co-operation.

Again, we stress that we have not set out to assemble some kind of "authorised version" of CND's development. However, we feel there is enough material here, from people who have been closely involved with the Campaign, to give many readers a better understanding of the movement's first twenty-five years. If this helps us all to work out our opposition to nuclear weapons more effectively in the years ahead, it will have been worthwhile.

John Minnion
Philip Bolsover
December 1982

INTRODUCTION

Any discussion of the Campaign for Nuclear Disarmament must begin with an extraordinary meeting in London on 17 February 1958. The Central Hall, Westminster, was booked, but it quickly became clear that this would be far too small: 5,000 people came and four overflow halls had to be used. Speakers were whisked from one hall to the next; they included Bertrand Russell, J.B. Priestley, Sir Stephen King-Hall, Canon John Collins and A.J.P. Taylor. CND had been launched.

The World has changed since that day twenty-five years ago; it has become more perilous, the shadow darker. And CND's aim, nuclear disarmament, is now more vital than ever. We reached our first peak in 1962; then we fought through the lean years of the late 1960s and early 1970s when, we were told, people were "learning to live with the Bomb"; and now, in numbers and influence, CND is a greater power than ever before – as it should be in these dangerous days.

At that first meeting, Bertrand Russell described how the whole human race was threatened by the reliance of a few politicians on a "balance" of nuclear weapons (the government had just reasserted its support for the Bomb, while admitting that "some unforeseen circumstances might spark off a world-wide catastrophe"). Speakers who emphasised clear moral rejection of nuclear weapons set the meeting alight. A.J.P. Taylor, the historian, described the effects of an H-bomb explosion and asked whether anyone present would want to inflict these on another human being. "Then why are we making the damned thing?" he demanded. The applause was deafening.

Afterwards, several hundred people marched from the meeting to Downing Street. It was a good-tempered crowd, but the police were worried; they came with dogs and made some arrests. *The Times* wrote an editorial about this incident but, like most papers, ignored the meeting. That has, by and large, been the attitude of the media ever since – though the horrible reality of our situation is now forcing a less frivolous, more concerned attitude, particularly from television.

The meeting had been set up by a brilliant organiser, the energetic, shrewd and humorous Peggy Duff, who for many years was the unsung heroine of the movement. Peggy was acting for an executive committee which had formally founded CND a month earlier. The committee brought to the Central Hall meeting a policy statement that did not clearly demand unilateral nuclear disarmament by Britain. But the audience wanted something tougher, and on the following day the statement was rewritten. As it set the tone of CND policy from that date until now, it is worth printing in full:

J.B. Priestley and Bertrand Russell at the first CND meeting, Central Hall, Westminster, 1958. (*Photo:* Henry Grant.)

Peggy Duff, CND's first secretary and organiser, on the 1958 London–Aldermaston march.

The purpose of the Campaign is to press for a British initiative to reduce the nuclear peril and to stop the armaments race. We shall seek to persuade the British people that Britain must:

(a) renounce unconditionally the use or production of nuclear weapons, and refuse to allow their use by others in her defence;

(b) use her utmost endeavour to bring about negotiations at all levels for agreement to end the armaments race and to lead to a general disarmament convention;

(c) invite the co-operation of other nations, particularly non-nuclear powers, in the renunciation of nuclear weapons.

So CND was on its way. Where was it going? As April Carter, Mervyn Jones and John Brunner explain (Chapter 1), one of the first places it was off to was the Aldermaston Weapons Research Establishment, where nuclear bombs were being designed. But where had CND come from? How and why did it start at that moment? Of course there are different views. A brief look at earlier events may suggest some explanations.

Origins

As early as 1943, Bob Edwards, later a Labour MP, wrote a pamphlet warning of the possible development of an atomic bomb. In 1945, when the A-bombs were used against Hiroshima and Nagasaki, many people were dismayed and horrified. But a majority of the nation, weary of war with Japan, no doubt shared the government's view, expressed by Churchill, that the Bomb seemed like "a miracle of deliverance". Christopher Driver in *The Disarmers* recalled that in 1945 only 21 per cent of the British disapproved of the nuclear bombing of Japan.

In 1950 the most prominent British peace campaign, the British Peace Committee, claimed more than a million signatures to the Stockholm Peace Appeal. The Appeal included these words:

We demand unconditional probibition of the atomic weapon as a weapon of aggression and mass annihilation of people, and that strict international control for the implementation of this decision be established. We shall consider as a war criminal that government which first employs atomic weapons against any country.

But many were blind to the merits of this appeal because it was backed by the Communist-led World Peace Conference. The Labour Party even added the BPC to its list of proscribed organisations.

Other moves were under way in 1950. In January, America had announced that she would develop the hydrogen bomb, many times more powerful than the A-bomb. Bishop Barnes, of Birmingham, demanded that Britain should not follow suit; a hundred Cambridge scientists petitioned the government to the same effect; and a number of religious and pacifist groups rallied three thousand people to a Hiroshima Day commemoration in Trafalgar Square. With Russia now armed with atomic weapons, civil defence came under attack – the Peace Pledge Union sold 45,000 copies of Dr Alex Comfort's critical leaflet *Civil Defence: What You Should Do Now*. The Peace Pledge Union had also set up a Non-Violence Commission in 1949 to explore the possibility of direct action to achieve a number of objectives: these included stopping the manufacture of atomic weapons in Britain. The resulting "Operation Gandhi" produced a token sit-down when eleven people were arrested outside the War Office in January 1952. It also produced, soon afterwards, what was probably the first demonstration at Aldermaston, where the research establishment was then being built. Only thirty people took part, but the seeds of the later Direct Action Committee were sown.

The manufacture and testing of bombs continued. In October 1952 Britain tested her first A-bomb; in November, America tried a 10-megaton H-bomb (equal in explosive power to 10 million tons of high explosive – far more than the total power of all the explosives used by all sides in the Second World War); and in August 1953 Russia tested her first H-bomb. Most traumatic of all was the US H-bomb test at Bikini Atoll in the Pacific, during March 1954. A Japanese fishing boat eighty-five miles away was contaminated by radioactive fallout from the bomb; all the crew were sick and one died.

In April 1954, a new movement was started – the Hydrogen Bomb National Campaign. Six Labour MPs met three hundred representatives from church, peace and labour organisations and launched a petition aiming at a million signatures by the end of the year. Local groups were formed and the million signatures were collected. Unfortunately, the petition called only for a top level disarmament conference and the strengthening of the United Nations; its terms were identical to a Labour Party opposition motion in the House of Commons, and even acceptable to the government, which continued to develop the British H-bomb. At the end of the year, this campaign was wound up.

A local action that year was more significant. Coventry City Council disbanded its Civil Defence Committee on the grounds that it was "a waste of time and public money". Again, seeds were being sown. Twenty-six years later, local councils all over the country began to declare themselves nuclear-free zones with the backing of CND, and were largely responsible for forcing the government to cancel the Hard Rock civil-defence exercise.

At the beginning of 1955 the government at last officially confirmed plans to make a British H-bomb. The Labour Opposition supported this "pending world disarmament". Aneurin Bevan abstained, along with seventy other Labour MPs, from supporting government policy – but without clearly rejecting a British H-bomb on any terms.

In July 1955, Bertrand Russell and Albert Einstein issued a manifesto signed by eleven internationally prominent scientists, nine of them Nobel prizewinners, who described the massive genetic damage that could be caused by nuclear weapons. The manifesto concluded: "Shall we put an end to the human race, or shall mankind renounce war?"

A few months earlier, a much less spectacular occasion had been attended by a retired civil servant, Christian and ex-suffragette called Gertrude Fishwick. Christopher Driver wrote:

> If any single person can be said to have triggered off the chain reaction which ended in CND it is Miss Fishwick, who died exhausted by her efforts two days before the Central Hall meeting which launched CND in 1958.

Gertrude Fishwick attended a meeting of the Women's Co-operative Guild at Golders Green in March 1955, where the radiation risks from H-bomb tests were discussed. As a result, she started and ran the Golders Green Committee for the Abolition of Nuclear Weapons Tests. Similar groups sprang up, first in neighbouring suburbs and then across the country. In February 1957, a National Committee for the Abolition of Nuclear Weapons Tests (NCANWT) was formed to co-ordinate the efforts of what, by the end of that year, were more than a hundred local groups.

The first British H-bomb tests were planned for the spring of 1957 at Christmas Island, in the Pacific. Opposition MPs pleaded for a postponement, and the British Council of Churches condemned the tests. In April, Duncan Sandys produced the government's Defence White Paper which said:

> It must be frankly recognised that there is at present no means of providing adequate protection for the people of this country against the consequences of an attack with nuclear weapons.

His conclusion was that "pending international agreement" the only safeguard for Britain against attack was to threaten retaliation with nuclear weapons. So the policy of British nuclear "deterrence" became official and, to our cost, remains the basis of defence policy to this day.

Opposition to the tests was spreading. In February 1957 two Quakers, Sheila and Harold Steele, had responded to a suggestion that a boat should be sailed into the Christmas Island test area, and in April the Direct Action Committee (DAC) was formed to support the enterprise. As it turned out, the boat was too late, but it attracted world-wide publicity.

That summer, the issue of the H-bomb was revived in the Labour Party. Thirty Labour MPs joined a new Labour H-bomb Campaign Committee and in September rallied 4,000 people in Trafalgar Square to oppose British manufacture of the Bomb. More ambitiously, a composite resolution proposing British unilateral renunciation of nuclear weapons was put to Labour's annual conference. Aneurin Bevan, in a now legendary speech, helped to crush the resolution.

It may be worth recalling a little of what Bevan said, since it has passed into nuclear folklore. First, he said that to strip Britain of nuclear weapons would be to send any British Foreign Secretary "naked into the conference chamber". He was speaking more than twenty-five years ago about a disarmament conference; but, naked or not, no progress in disarmament has been made since. He pointed to the possibility of unilateral nuclear disarmament in the future:

> Action of that sort will still be there available to us if our other actions fail. It is something you can always do. You can always, if the influence you have upon your allies and your opponents is not yielding any fruits, take unilateral action of that sort.

In November 1957 a *New Statesman* article, "Britain and the Nuclear Bombs" by J.B. Priestley, drew such a massive response from readers that Kingsley Martin, the editor, proposed a meeting with the idea of starting a mass movement against nuclear weapons. NCANWT seemed the most promising base, so the sponsors and officers of this committee were invited to the meeting at the house of Canon John Collins, of St Paul's Cathedral, with a number of others – about fifty altogether – on 16 January 1958. They included Bertrand Russell; Rose Macauley, the novelist; Sir Julian Huxley; Bishop Bell, of Chichester; Michael Foot; Sir Richard Acland; Ritchie Calder; James Cameron; and, importantly, from NCANWT, Arthur Goss, its Quaker chairman, Dr Sheila Jones, and Peggy Duff, who had convened the meeting. NCANWT agreed to transfer its funds, its staff of three, its offices and files, and even its booking of Central Hall, Westminster, for 17 February, to a new body – the Campaign for Nuclear Disarmament – with aims extending far beyond a ban on nuclear weapons tests. Bertrand Russell became president and Peggy Duff organising secretary. The shift from campaigning simply against nuclear weapons tests to opposing the weapons themselves clearly reflected the mood of the movement. All but one of NCANWT's local groups became CND groups.

A second vital initiative had started in November 1957. The DAC met to welcome Harold Steele back from Japan and discuss future plans. Hugh Brock, editor of *Peace News* and organiser of the 1952 Aldermaston demonstration, suggested a four-day march to Aldermaston for Easter 1958, and in December an *ad hoc* Aldermaston march committee was set up, with Pat Arrowsmith, from NCANWT, as organiser, Frank Allaun, MP, Hugh Brock and Walter Wolfgang, then organiser of the Labour Hydrogen-Bomb Campaign Comittee. In January 1958 CND's new executive agreed to "give its blessing" to the march "but should make it clear at this stage of the Campaign that they could not be very closely involved". Apart from anything else, the Campaign had not yet held its first meeting.

The first year

The attitudes of these founding groups were important – though not so important as the responses of the thousands who flocked into the movement. The perspective of the DAC is indicated by April Carter in Chapter 1. CND clearly presented itself as a single-issue campaign, as J.B. Priestley's early "Statement of Policy" leaflet shows:

> The Campaign for Nuclear Disarmament seeks to persuade people that the atomic and similar armaments are totally wrong and should be abolished, and it has no other aim. But its members believe that mere vague condemnation of atomic weapons is not enough, and that some definite action must be taken. The British Government should announce its intention to abolish these armaments, and should then proceed to do so, at a given date, whatever other nuclear powers may decide. One nation able to produce these weapons should set other nations an example by deliberately challenging the hysterical fear that is behind the arms race ... And Britain cannot be adequately defended by atomic armaments. To retain them, to keep on manufacturing them, at a cost that menaces our whole economy, is merely to play an idiotic game of bluff.

Priestley was at that time vice-president of CND.

Canon Collins spoke of a "short, sharp campaign", and certainly most of those who set up CND assumed that its aims would be achieved by winning over the Labour Party and then helping that party to victory. Yet, ironically, both at the big initial meeting and at meetings during the first Aldermaston march the most popular speeches showed scepticism toward all political parties.

The new movement could not be explained in orthodox political terms. It was not a Communist organisation; in fact the Communist Party kept to the multilaterist line and did not swing behind CND until 1960. Nor was it immediately supported by all pacifists; some felt it did not go far enough. But at last people were beginning to realise the sheer horror and magnitude of nuclear weapons. Early in 1958, a Gallup poll showed that 80 per cent of the British public expected less than half of Britain's population to survive a nuclear war. The issue was – and still is – survival.

There were also immediate issues in those early months. In February 1958 Britain finally signed an agreement with the USA to build four bases in East Anglia for sixty Thor missiles, nuclear-armed with a 1,500-mile range. Opinion polls had already shown majority opposition in Britain to these bases. The analogy with Cruise missiles in the 1980s is uncanny. In March that year, NATO decided that West Germany must be armed with tactical nuclear weapons. The *Guardian* reported a protest rally on 23 March in Frankfurt 20,000 strong. Christopher Driver later wrote of 120,000 people protesting in Hamburg that year. In addition, nuclear weapons tests in 1958 were reaching a record level: almost 100 in one year – double the 1957 figure, which in turn had been double that of 1956.

During CND's first year, action against the Bomb took many forms, came from many quarters. We often make too glib a contrast between 1958 and 1980. Certainly, since 1980 the vital impetus for CND's resurgence has come from local, diverse and often quite specific campaigns. But already in 1958 the very diversity of the movement was a source of strength. There was an exhilarating sense of co-operation with thousands of others for a common purpose.

The first Aldermaston march (described by Mervyn Jones and John Brunner in Chapter 1) showed this co-operation at its best. That march brought a by-product that has achieved world-wide fame: the CND symbol. Gerald Holtom, a professional artist and member of Twickenham CND, was the originator. He explained later that his first thoughts on the need for a symbol flowed from the practical difficulty of making large banners with the cumbersome phrase "Unilateral Nuclear Disarmament" written on them! The symbol is a composite of the semaphore signal for the letters N and D. Holtom also saw in the central motif an indication of a human being in despair; the circle represented the world, the black background eternity. Eric Austen, who made the first badge version of the symbol, subsequently found that the "gesture of despair" motif has historically represented the death of man, and the circle the unborn child. The symbol was first adopted for use on the 1958 march by Pat Arrowsmith and Hugh Brock. Of course it has since been used to symbolise nuclear disarmament, peace and related causes all over the world, and was even banned in South Africa in 1974.

An independent move came from the Nuclear Disarmament Mass Lobby Committee. Within a month of the Easter Aldermaston March they had organised a lobby of Parliament estimated as up to 10,000 strong. In June an all-women rally, "Women Against the Bomb", was virtually ignored by the press, but it was, by all accounts, a moving occasion. Jacquetta Hawkes wrote to several papers saying:

> ... It could well start a women's movement against Britain's nuclear armaments at least as powerful as the movement for women's suffrage. ... It seems that so long as we women are trivial, we are assured of space in the press: when we are deeply serious over a matter of life and death we are ignored.

As Alison Whyte indicates (Chapter 4), women in the 1980s may fulfil that hope.

By spring 1959, 270 public meetings had been organised, often with impressive "star" bills. Over the same period the number of groups inherited from NCANWT more than doubled. "Specialist" sections were set up, like the Scientists' Group (a forerunner of the present successful SANA) and even an Architects' Group, which produced exhibitions, designed, made and did running repairs on hundreds of banners!

In January 1959, CND took another first step, this time in a direction which pointed the way towards the European Nuclear Disarmament Movement of the 1980s. A conference was held, partly in London and partly in Frankfurt, which led to the establishment of a European Federation Against Nuclear Arms. This included movements in Britain, Holland, West Germany and Sweden. Peggy Duff recalled the limitations of the Federation. One was the refusal of the West Germans to have any dialogue at all with Russians or East Europeans, for fear of being seen as pro-Communist. Another was a "ration" of two organisations from each country, which, with other restrictions, was designed to keep out direct-action organisations.

By the end of 1958, the Direct Action Committee was once more in British headlines with the Swaffham Thor base demonstration described by April Carter in Chapter 1. Canon Collins issued a statement dissociating CND from civil disobedience, but many campaigners were unhappy about this and the executive was forced to modify its position. Civil disobedience was a major issue at CND's first annual conference in March 1959.

As CND became more influential it was confronted with another problem: tactics in parliamentary and local elections. More than twenty years later, the problem remains, and an indication of the arguments in these earlier debates is useful today. In 1958 a London University Students' Committee proposed a "Voters Veto" – a campaign against votes for any parliamentary candidate who did not support CND policy. The Campaign's executive consistently opposed this, but agreed to have the arguments stated in the CND Bulletin.

Michael Foot put the case against the Voters' Veto. He called it a "policy for hermits", arguing: "Only through the election of a Labour Government and the political pressure which we may exert afterwards can we succeed."

Michael Craft, chairman of the Colleges and Universities CND, argued for the Veto: "The greatest tragedy for the Campaign would be the return of a Labour Government with its policy unchanged. It is pious to hope that we could change their policy in office, and disillusion would spread in the Campaign. The great merit of the Voters' Veto is to force the Labour Party to think again before it is too late." Many people may feel that Michael Craft's scepticism was justified by later events.

Voter's Veto was soon put to the test when, in early 1959, there was a by-election in S.W. Norfolk, where the Labour candidate, who opposed CND policy, won with a slightly increased majority. After that, Voters' Veto faded for lack of results – but the problem did not go away.

The general outlook for CND was encouraging. There were now nearly 300 local groups, and public opinion polls showed that support for a British Ban-the-Bomb policy had risen from 25 per cent in April 1958 to 30 per cent in March 1959. Internationally, a moratorium (though not a ban) on nuclear tests had just started.

At this stage, CND decided to hold a second Easter March, but to reverse the direction. The march would start at Aldermaston instead of ending there, and would conclude with a great demonstration in Trafalgar Square. Despite some doubts, more people than ever turned up in Falcon Field, opposite the main entrance to the Weapons Research Establishment, fifty miles from London. The London Co-op Party loudspeaker van — surely one of the quietest ever — croaked out an inter-denominational service, and off they went: jazz bands and guitars, songs and slogans, banners, placards and pamphlets. Adrian Henri and Ian Campbell recall in Chapter 6 some moments from those Aldermaston years.

The logistics were no joke. Jo Richardson (Chapter 1) describes the problems of catering without experience for unknown numbers. Then there were luggage vans, banner wagons, litter collectors and Elsan toilet teams; stewards, dispatch riders, first-aid teams ... the list is endless. But the problems were problems of success, of providing for thousands instead of hundreds, and when 20,000 people crowded into Trafalgar Square on Easter Monday 1959 it was the Campaign's biggest rally. In later years the annual Easter march — and headcount — may have become a millstone round the movement's neck; and some local CND groups may have become frustrated by seeing themselves mainly as recruiting posts for the big demonstrations (in the 1980s, local groups seem to have a much firmer base in local campaigning); but the early marches, as Peter Worsley writes (Chapter 6) were the means by which the movement first got to know itself.

Over the next five years, three tactical questions concerned CND, and the response to each affected the others. First, how should the Campaign relate to parliamentary politics? Second, how should it relate to the direct action wing of the movement? Third, how could it best consolidate its own identity in terms of policy, organisation and activity?

Parliamentary politics

CND had set out to convince people "from all political parties and none" that nuclear disarmament should be made an absolute priority. In 1959, none of the major political parties supported CND policy though, as Robert Fyson shows in Chapter 7, the Liberals probably came nearest. This and other articles by David Griffiths and Isobel Lindsay (Chapter 7) and Frank Allaun (Chapter 2) suggest how the Campaign's relationship with the political parties could now, in the 1980s, be more productive; and there is also the emergence of the smaller, though fully anti-nuclear Ecology Party. But Andrew Papworth explains in Chapter 7 some of the reasons why many campaigners have become wary of being "smothered" by party politics.

In the 1959 general election, the Campaign's advice to CND local groups was as tentative as the Voters' Veto appeal had been uncompromising. It was to:

> Support any candidates considered to be genuine supporters of CND, but to pay due respect to, and recognise, the existence of the party allegiances of individual members.

With Labour and Conservative nuclear weapons politics virtually identical, defence was hardly an issue in the 1959 election. Labour lost, but there was at least a minority of about seventy Labour MPs who would support CND to the point of abstaining on some defence votes. (In 1961, five Labour MPs, including Michael Foot, were, in fact, expelled from the Parliamentary Labour Party for voting against the Conservative government's Defence Estimates.)

A more important consequence of the 1959 election was perhaps that, with no conference that year, the 1960 Labour Party conference vote in favour of unilateral nuclear disarmament seemed a more sudden change of policy than it really was. Hugh Gaitskell, the party leader, made his famous declaration that he would "fight, fight and fight again" to reverse the decision, and, as Frank Allaun explains (Chapter 2), in 1961 the unilateral disarmament vote was duly reversed.

By the following year a new group, the Independent Nuclear Disarmament Election Committee (INDEC), had been launched, but on the Aldermaston march that year it handed out a leaflet saying that it had "no wish to divide the Campaign by urging official backing". It put up Michael Craft in the 1964 election and he received 1,000 votes. Clearly, by fighting on what was basically a one-plank platform, INDEC under-represented CND's public support.

At the 1964 election, CND once more set out to establish an "independent presence"; it again drew up lists of candidates who were pro-CND and encouraged support for them. Questions were asked at election meetings; the Campaign organised forums on defence policy with candidates speaking and conducted various other activities. But work was patchy.

Basking in the rather limited glory of the Partial Test Ban Treaty, the Conservatives still declared that Britain should have her own nuclear weapons. This made it much easier for the Labour and Liberal Parties to sound radical by simply opposing *British* nuclear weapons, particularly our Polaris submarines, while accepting full participation in NATO's nuclear weapons strategy. After the election Harold Wilson's government ignored even this commitment.

The direct-action debate

The tendency of some CND leaders to think exclusively in terms of winning over the Labour Party did not help the unity of the Campaign. In particular it strengthened the polarisation over direct action.

The articles in Chapter 8 suggest some changing of attitudes on direct action; but earlier articles, for instance those by Norman and Janey Buchan (Chapter 1), John Petherbridge (Chapter 2) and Adrian Henri (Chapter 6), illustrate the way in which many individual disarmers always saw the activities of CND and the Committee of 100 as very much a part of the same campaign. The early debates on this subject are, of course, very relevant to the 1980s — sometimes startlingly so.

As well as having principled doubts, CND's leaders were anxious about the public impact of any form of direct action that involved breaking the law. Canon Collins records that though he felt individuals should be left free to act according to conscience:

> It seemed to me that for CND as such to identify itself with illegalities would be to alienate its potential supporters, not only in the Labour movement but outside it, to whom the bulk of campaigners wished to address themselves.

In many people's view this was, and is, a reasonable anxiety: if direct action takes a form that loses us support in the country then it is surely hard to justify, except perhaps in an extreme emergency. But an immediate issue at the end of the 1950s was the Thor missile bases — an obvious parallel with Cruise missiles in the 1980s — and these bases had been opposed by a majority in the opinion polls. And the non-violent action at the Swaffham base in 1958 had seemed to meet a sympathetic response from at least a section of the public. On 2 January 1960, a successful formula was found for CND and the Direct-Action Committee to co-operate in a demonstration at the Harrington Thor base. CND organised a supporting march past the base where the DAC had planned a sit-down. Inevitably, the two sections became entangled, but Peggy Duff describes how even the police seemed to want the two wings of the movement to co-exist.

> Anxious to arrest only those who had come there for that purpose, they walked around asking people if they wanted to be arrested. If the answer was "no", they passed on; if the answer was "yes", they obliged.

Eighty-two DAC supporters were arrested in this strange compromise event.

Then came the Committee of 100 with its idea of mass civil disobedience, and its cry of "Fill the jails". Two early and important converts were Bertrand Russell and the Rev. Michael Scott, both also founder members of CND and sponsors of the DAC. At this stage, there was no difference between the policies of CND and those of the Committee of 100; the argument was solely about the means to be used.

The original Committee drew in prominent figures from the world of entertainment and the arts, including John Arden, Shelagh Delaney, Lindsay Anderson, John Braine, Augustus John, Robin Hall, George Melly, John Neville, John Osborne, Herbert Read and Arnold Wesker.

Canon Collins, chairman of CND, was distressed that Russell had not warned him of the plans for the new organisation, and it was unfortunate that incidents surrounding the formation of the Committee caused dangerous personal frictions between the two men.

By the time the Committee of 100 was officially launched on 25 October 1960, Bertrand Russell had resigned from the presidency of CND on the grounds that he could not work with Canon Collins as chairman.

Matters had to improve; and they did. The Committee of 100's first demonstration, on 18 February 1961, was entirely non-violent; it brought 4,000 people to sit down outside the Ministry of Defence – with no arrests. More important, it was timed to coincide with the arrival of *Proteus*, the US Polaris depot ship, in Holy Loch, Scotland. The sit-down, together with the DAC's symbolic canoe-borne resistance to the ship's arrival, caught the public's imagination. In March 1961, CND's annual conference reaffirmed the Campaign's own commitment to legal methods but congratulated the organisers of these demonstrations on their timing, and accepted that the methods of the DAC, the Committee of 100 and CND must be seen as "three techniques in a united attack on preparations for nuclear war".

Russell outlined his arguments for civil disobedience in a speech in Birmingham. He laid much emphasis on the publicity value; the main reason why they could not be content with ordinary methods of political propaganda was that:

> so long as only constitutional methods were employed, it was very difficult – and often impossible – to cause the most important facts to be known. All the great newspapers are against us. Television and radio gave us only grudging and brief opportunities for stating our case. Politicians who opposed us were reported in full, while those who supported us were dubbed "hysterical" ... It was very largely the difficulty of making our case known that drove some of us to the adoption of illegal methods ...

But the Committee's illegal actions were reported because they had sensational news value,

> and here and there a newspaper would allow us to say why we did what we did. ... Not only was our demonstration of 18 February widely reported in every part of the world, but as an immediate consequence, all sorts of newspapers printed statements of our case which, until then, they would have rejected.

The high point of the Committee's activity came in September 1961.

Simultaneous sit-downs were planned for Battle of Britain Sunday at Holy Loch and in Trafalgar Square. At the beginning of September the government acted in a way that gave the London sit-downs maximum publicity. Thirty-six prominent members of the Committee were summoned to Bow Street magistrates' court and ordered to bind themselves over to keep the peace – apparently sitting down could be an action likely to cause a breach of the peace. Thirty-two, including the 89-year-old Bertrand Russell and his wife, refused, and most were sentenced to prison for two months (reduced to one week for Russell when he showed a medical certificate).

This brought a wave of public sympathy for the demonstration in an atmosphere already affected by renewed nuclear weapons tests by both America and Russia; and there was an East-West crisis over Berlin which prompted the now infamous statement by Sir Alec Home, the Foreign Secretary: "The British people are prepared to be blown to atomic dust if necessary."

Thousands came to Trafalgar Square and 1,314 were arrested, including, ironically, Canon Collins and some other CND "observers". During the same weekend, 351 were arrested at Holy Loch.

The next big Committee of 100 demonstration was on 9 December at Wethersfield United States Air Force base, with simultaneous actions at Brize Norton and Ruislip bases and supporting demonstrations in Bristol, Cardiff, York and Manchester. Despite the arrest of six organisers under the Official Secrets Act, on 8 December, about 5,000 joined the various activities and more than 800 were arrested. In the following February, five of the arrested organisers were sentenced to eighteen months in prison and one to twelve months.

During the ensuing months a network of regional Committee of 100 groups developed to run their own demonstrations. Here is one that strikes a familiar note: more than a hundred supporters of the Oxford Committee of 100 were arrested for attempting to immobilise Greenham Common air base in June 1962.

At the local level, CND and Committee members worked side by side, particularly in the week of the Cuba crisis at the end of October 1962. Soon after this, the Committee's activities and financial resources began to tail off, and it was finally wound up in 1968.

Meanwhile in CND ...

CND gradually consolidated its organisation and refined its policy, but to the public, campaigners were above all the people who ran the "Ban the Bomb!" marches in general and the annual Aldermaston marches in particular. These

Homeosaurus – Easter 1964. "Too much armour, too little brain.– now he's extinct."
(*Photo*: R.F. Gudd.)

Michael Foot, pushing his step-grandson, Jason Eohel, and accompanied by James Cameron, marches with the Ebbw Vale contingent in Trafalgar Square during the 1964 Easter demonstration. (*Photo:* The Sports and General Press Agency.)

became, unfortunately, the barometer by which the whole of the movement was gauged. But the number of groups (there was no national membership until 1966) was certainly a more accurate standard. By 1960 there were more than 450 groups, and at the peak, a year or so later, about double that number could be claimed. At this time the Campaign's national office employed about twenty people full-time, and half a dozen regional councils each had a full-time organiser. *Sanity*, the Campaign's monthly paper, had a circulation of 45,000 at its peak.

In terms of policy there were clarifications. Most important, the 1960 annual conference called for British withdrawal from any alliance based on the use of nuclear weapons. This meant rejecting NATO in particular, an implication that worried some supporters, but followed logically enough from the rejection of reliance on nuclear weapons.

The 1961 conference reaffirmed this policy of unilateral withdrawal from NATO by Britain, but went on to introduce the concept of positive neutralism (see Peter Worsley, Chapter 6). Though the particular formula may have varied over the years, the commitment to non-alignment and against nuclear alliances has remained part of the Campaign's policy ever since. (Opposition to weapons of mass destruction analogous to nuclear arms, in particular chemical and biological weapons, has been the other logical extension of CND policy which is surely here to stay.)

By 1962, while CND's basic policy demands were clear, the British government's nuclear policy was in considerable disarray. Only two years after the completion of the Thor bases, it was announced that they would be closed in 1963. Two British tactical-missile programmes, the surface-launched Blue Water and the air-launched TSR 2, were scrapped. And plans to buy Skybolt, an American air-launched missile, collapsed when the Americans cancelled this project. The British government's decision to build four submarines, fitted with the American Polaris missile system, was a last-ditch bid to stay in the nuclear missile race.

But the dominant political crisis of 1962 was in October over Cuba, where America confronted Russia with a nuclear threat to stop the Russians from building missile bases there. The crisis resolved itself mainly because it involved no vital national interest for Russia.

The 1962 Aldermaston march had been, *Sanity* claimed, the biggest of them all. *Peace News* estimated that 150,000 people were at the final rally, this time in Hyde Park. That Easter, *Sanity* reported that 200,000 marchers had taken part in forty-four demonstrations in fifteen countries (still a far cry from the huge numbers twenty years later). But the logistics were becoming a strain. For instance, 15,000 marchers had to be housed under canvas in Reading that year.

By the time of the Cuba crisis in October 1962, the Campaign was able to marshal "instant" marches all over the country, yet was not confident of their effectiveness. The media presented Cuba as evidence that the American deterrent had worked; so, it was implied, it would continue to work indefinitely. CND was able to point out that nuclear bases, far from protecting Cuba, had nearly got the island obliterated. The analogy with Britain's position was sound, but unheeded. Nigel Young (Chapter 2) discusses the impact of the Cuba crisis on the Campaign.

On Good Friday 1963, an anonymous group called, mysteriously, "Spies for Peace" distributed to the Aldermaston marchers a pamphlet that reported the results of a NATO exercise simulating a Russian attack on Britain – "Fallex". It also revealed not only the existence but the sites of the network of underground bunkers that would become Regional Seats of Government after a nuclear attack. Information about these matters is widely known in the 1980s, but at that time the news was sensational and was quoted in the newspapers. In theory, details of the RSGs were official secrets, though later the government (perhaps to save its face) said it had intended to publish the information in due course. Meanwhile, a more immediate effect of the "Spies" revelation was to heighten friction between some of the Campaign's national leadership and the direct-action wing of the movement over CND's image and tactics.

When the Partial Test Ban Treaty prohibiting nuclear tests in the atmosphere was signed in the summer of 1963, world leaders echoed CND's long-repeated warnings about the dangers of radiation. But to the extent that we had concentrated much of our attention on the immediate target of nuclear bomb testing, the Campaign lost some of its sense of urgency.

By autumn that year, CND had adopted a policy of co-operation between all wings of the movement in such exercises as Fallex-63. This was a nation-wide propaganda campaign to publish the results of the NATO Fallex-62 exercise by showing the damage that would be caused by such an attack. Posters were issued showing the effects in terms of radiation, firestorm, blast and the crater areas. The authorities were worried; in some areas police cars followed CND loudspeaker vans, and posters were removed by police from sites several times in succession during one evening.

Achievements: 1958-64

Perhaps this is a moment to assess the achievements of the first few years, for although the tide was ebbing there had indeed been considerable successes, and these formed the basis for much that is now beginning to be achieved.

First, the basic achievement: CND had brought nuclear weapons and their dangers from a shroud of semi-secrecy into the field of permanent public discussion. It was no longer possible to ignore the fact that this was the key to the future (or non-future) of mankind. On this everything, then and now, rested.

Second, the Campaign had informed people of the perils from radioactive fallout, and had contributed largely to the American-British-Soviet ban on nuclear weapons tests in the atmosphere – the Partial Test Ban Treaty, which undoubtedly saved many thousands of lives.

Third, the Campaign made an impact on all political parties in the debate about general disarmament; all the parties were forced at least to profess support for multilateral disarmament.

Fourth, the Campaign made the *official* policy of the Labour and Liberal Parties one of opposition to the British independent nuclear force – though this policy did not include withdrawal from NATO and, in fact, it was *not* put into practice by the Labour Party in office.

Fifth, as Canon Collins pointed out, it opened a dialogue between pacifists and concerned non-pacifists, brought together by the nuclear threat.

Sixth, and in some ways most important of all, it aroused the interest and enthusiasm of a whole generation of young people, giving them not only a base for political activity but also a forum for all kinds of fresh ideas. It widened the horizons of the young in a way probably unprecedented in British history. This was the generation that, largely through CND, became the foundation for virtually all radical movements in the next ten to twenty years. As early as Easter 1959, more than 40 per cent of the Aldermaston marchers were, according to an informal survey, under 21. This proportion increased in later marches. Their sons and daughters, with many more, are the strength of the revived Campaign in the 1980s. This aspect of the Campaign is so widespread in its influence as to be incalculable.

The problem years

Signs of the lull in public support for CND became fully apparent in 1964. Considered in the long term, however, this was temporary, and it has been followed by a surge of support even greater than that which accompanied the founding of the Campaign. And although backing for CND's public activity fell off, widespread and enormous goodwill for the movement remained.

In retrospect, CND's early emphasis on nuclear weapons tests diverted attention from the more important and fundamental demand for the abolition of the weapons themselves. The world-wide spread of radioactive fallout from bomb tests in the atmosphere, and the well publicised evidence of links between fallout and cancer and other diseases brought an enormous number of people into the Campaign. When the Partial Test Ban Treaty was signed, many supporters, thinking the main battle was won, retired from the fray. But of course the fight was only just beginning. The tests did not stop; they merely went underground – more of them than ever – and nuclear weapons piled up at an increasing rate. Nevertheless, some people were, to quote an unpleasant phrase widely used at the time, "learning to live with the Bomb". Only later did new developments make clear that it was impossible to live unconcerned in a world increasingly threatened by nuclear terror.

From the first days of CND, Canon Collins had talked of a "short, sharp campaign" to force the adoption of a governmental ban on nuclear bombs in this country. But after five years the phrase wore thin. The most enthusiastic and hard-working supporters of CND, the Campaign's shock troops, had worked unceasingly; now some of them began to tire.

Added to this was disillusionment with the Labour Party. From the beginning, a large section of the Campaign had based its hope and activity on work within the Labour Party for the election of a government that would scrap British nuclear weapons and lead the world towards general nuclear disarmament. But when Labour won the 1964 election Harold Wilson's government killed any hope that it would follow an anti-nuclear policy. The Polaris programme continued; nuclear bases remained and were extended; Americans continued to man their nuclear outposts in Britain. In the later 1960s, the Wilson government made a superficial move to defuse opposition to nuclear weapons by mothballing civil defence for the time being, but this was not impressive.

The Easter 1964, one-day march in London may have numbered as few as 20,000 people; and even this was rather better than the average of subsequent years. During the summer of that year, Youth CND renewed a different approach. Going to where crowds were, and people had leisure to talk and listen, they organised "On the Beach" campaigns with CND rock, donkey rides and "non-violent" Punch and Judy shows at seaside holiday towns!

In 1964, when the lean years of the Campaign were beginning, the future leader of the Labour Party, Michael Foot, wrote: " ... if there was no CND in existence now, it would be necessary to invent it." Referring to the "world-wide debate" about nuclear weapons and their perils, he asked:

Is this a debate which everyone should join in, or is it one to be left to the experts, the scientists who know, the military advisers, the very few? The differing responses to that question go to the roots of our democracy and our political system.

He referred to CND's "most explosive point", its distinctive contribution – the demand for unilateral nuclear disarmament by Britain:

No one can deny the plain fact. CND developed differently from the campaigns that had gone before, provoked furious enthusiasms and enmities, and made a spectacular appeal to the young, precisely because it did not take refuge in vague generalities, precisely because it did urge that something could be done, precisely because it did pin responsibility on our country, on us.

Michael Foot was writing two years after he had left the executive of the Campaign. Indeed, by 1964 most of the "famous names" had left CND. Their activity, when considered in relation to the Campaign's twenty-five years of work, was regrettably ephemeral. One criticism of CND during its early years was that it was dominated by middle-class supporters and "star" names – that it lacked active, working support from, for instance, the rank and file of the trade unions and other organisations of the working class. Although the national conferences of several trade unions passed resolutions backing CND, and although national figures like Frank Cousins, secretary of the Transport and General Workers' Union, did much valuable work, there was never a widespread attempt by sympathetic unions to generate activity among the mass of their membership. In fact, CND itself did little in practical terms directly to increase such activity.

But it is interesting that what support there was in the trade unions remained solid during CND's lean years. Indeed, as middle-class support fell away and young people, particularly the students, dispersed into radical organisations of various kinds, or made community projects and alternative life-styles their priority, support among rank-and-file union members tended to increase. It was perhaps significant that in 1970, when the Campaign was at a low ebb in terms of explicit public support, the Easter March (from Crawley New Town to Trafalgar Square was partly organised by Crawley Trades Council and headed by the Council's banner. The slogan "Ban the Bomb – Cut the Arms Bill" was allied to emphasis on the adverse effect of arms expenditure on the social services. On the other hand, there was not yet adequate CND attention to one problem that troubled some trade unionists: the effect of arms cuts on the employment of people in industries related to arms manufacture. The reply to that question became more urgent in subsequent years as unemployment rapidly increased.

By 1965, America's war in Vietnam was dominating the thoughts of many people involved in the peace movement. Naturally, this affected CND. There were many long and heart-searching debates about the way the Campaign should relate to the Vietnam protests. This was the most serious challenge that CND had yet faced on the question of how far it should interest itself in a matter outside its normal sphere. It could be said that the Vietnam war was capable of becoming a conflict in which nuclear weapons would be used, either in a clash between the superpowers or by America alone as part of her military effort against her Vietnamese opponents. This point was part of the argument – but only part – pressed by many Campaigners who wanted to see peace in Vietnam become CND's main priority; the Campaign was, after all, still Britain's biggest peace organisation. The opposition argument was that CND should stick to its prime purpose, and that it would weaken itself by diverting energy to the Peace in Vietnam movement.

Undoubtedly the horrors of American activities in Vietnam did divert attention from the even greater horrors and the universal threat to the human race implicit in the nuclear arms race. As the months passed, many CND supporters became absorbed in the "Save Vietnam" movement. Peggy Duff, the mainspring of CND so far as any one person could be, had no doubts about involving the Campaign, and the majority of the National Council took the same view, though there were always doubters. But pacifists in CND had additional doubts; they could not, naturally, support the armed struggle of the Vietnamese, and they preferred to back Buddhist attempts to secure a peaceful settlement.

John Cox, the longest serving chairman of CND, wrote in *Overkill*, a basic document for anyone interested in the Campaign:

> ... most members of CND were forthright in their opposition to the US intervention, but did not want the Campaign to pass opinions on the internal politics of Vietnam. The policy they favoured most was British dissociation from US policy in Vietnam and support for the right of the Vietnamese people to settle their own affairs free from foreign interference.

In 1965, 1966 and 1967, CND did campaign on the Vietnam issue. In local and national demonstrations, posters and banners calling for an end to nuclear arms were freely interspersed with demands for peace in Vietnam and attacks on US bombing of that country. The 1966 Trafalgar Square Easter rally had a giant puppet show on the Vietnam war and British government complicity. Adrian Mitchell and Michael Kustow wrote the script, Gerald Scarfe designed 20-foot-high puppets, and John Wells was the main "voice". Mass opposition to the war was later led by the Vietnam Solidarity Campaign, organised by Tariq Ali and others, and then by the British Campaign for Peace in Vietnam, a less strident organisation. There was some criticism when Dick Nettleton, who had succeeded Peggy Duff as CND general secretary, also became for a time the BCPV's first secretary, but the relations between the two bodies remained close, and for some time BCPV shared a room with *Sanity* in the CND office.

"This relationship," wrote John Cox, "set a pattern for a more co-operative style of working with other organisations ... It also showed how to handle the problem of side issues – by working with other organisations when campaign objectives overlapped, rather than attempting to broaden CND's goals." In the 1980s a similar approach was applied to relations with the World

Disarmament Campaign, organised by two remarkable veterans, Lord Brockway and Lord Noel Baker; and to European Nuclear Disarmament, with Edward Thompson as its leading figure: END was accommodated in an enlarged CND office in 1982.

By 1966 there was an addition to the nuclear-armed nations – China exploded an H-bomb. This brought demonstrators to the Chinese Embassy in London with a letter of protest. It was a strange affair with an element of black humour. A deputation carrying the letter repeatedly rang the Embassy doorbell, and then, getting no reply, pushed the letter into the letter box. Promptly, the letter came flying back, projected by an unseen hand. This process was repeated several times, until suddenly the door opened. The deputation entered a lobby to be confronted by a row of figures, one of whom addressed the protesters at some length. The Chinese listened silently to the deputation's reply, thrust aside the proffered letter, offered little red books and with two or three gentle but firm shoves in the direction of the door, indicated that the visit was over.

In 1966 CND finally introduced a national membership scheme: after the prolonged debate on the principle, it was financial necessity that clinched the decision.

Also in 1966, CND demonstrated at Barrow-in-Furness against the launch of the first vessel in Britain's Polaris submarine fleet by the Queen Mother. Albert Booth, MP for Barrow, declined to attend the ceremony and marched with the protesters instead. The launch of the second Polaris submarine was the occasion for another demonstration. This time, the Bishop of Chester refused to bless the vessel; he was rebuked by Dennis Healey, Defence Minister, with the strange statement that to offer a blessing was "a matter of political judgement, not moral judgement". The third launch at Barrow in 1967, and the fourth at Birkenhead in 1968 were also the subject of demonstrations.

Steps toward revival

During the next four years there were marches of various kinds and sizes; four-day marches, two-day, one-day; marches from Aldermaston again, and even one *to* Aldermaston like the very first. But more and more the Campaign turned to other forms of activity and propaganda. These were to some extent forced on CND by declining numbers, but they were welcomed by a majority of the National Council and proved an important development in CND's history.

The Easter march from Crawley (Sussex) to London in 1970 attracted a comparatively small number of people, but a "Festival for Life", in Victoria Park, Hackney, the following day was a great success, with 20,000 people there. The festival was initiated by a small group of campaigners anxious to move away from "Trafalgar Square-ism", and it showed a welcome tolerance of diverse approaches in the re-awakening peace movement. It began to build on the anti-war mood of recent rock music festivals, particularly the big events at the Isle of Wight and at Woodstock, in America (rock bands were now returning from the US with CND symbols painted on their instruments). The theme of the festival, peace and the abolition of nuclear weapons, came across in a variety of ways. There were five stages accommodating rock bands and jazz bands, folk music, poets reading their own and other peoples' works, and variety turns of various kinds. In the crowds, street theatre groups organised by Joan Littlewood and others, performed. On one stage, John Peel conducted a telephone interview with John Lennon. All sections of the peace movement had stalls, and it was here and in many side shows that much effective propaganda was done.

A similar Easter festival at Alexandra Park, London, in the following year was even more varied and successful. A play written for the occasion – *Passion* by Edward Bond – was performed by actors of the English Stage Company, and support for CND by other groups was stronger than ever.

In 1972 a four-day march to Aldermaston ended with a festival in Falcon Field, opposite the main gate of the nuclear weapons research establishment. (Hawkwind were among the bands that year, playing through a modest 600 watts p.a. system). The affirmation of life and opposition to nuclear weapons at the gates of an establishment devoted to universal death was moving and effective. Adrian Henri (Chapter 6) recalls some moments from these festivals.

By 1973 first signs of CND's revival were appearing in Scotland, where the presence of British and US Polaris submarines only 30 miles from Glasgow and the most thickly populated area of the country, was a constant reminder of the nuclear threat (Ian Davison, Chapter 3). Both here and in the rest of Britain the emphasis of the Campaign was moving more and more to local activity as the 1970s passed, with "weeks of action", town demonstrations, meetings, pressure on MPs and showings of *The War Game*, the film of a possible nuclear attack on Britain, made by Peter Watkins for BBC television and then banned by them. Another influential film *All Against the Bomb* was made by CND for the BBC's Open Door series (Chapter 3, Duncan Rees), and at the start of the 1980s, the ITV film *The Bomb*, made by Jonathan Dimbleby, has proved an eloquent successor to these. The Campaign's increased emphasis on "education" was reflected during the 1970s in a steady flow of influential pamphlets by David Griffiths, Zoë Fairbairns, Dan Smith, John Cox and others.

Two additional developments in the 1970s were the decision of the Campaign to increase its opposition to chemical and biological weapons (reflected in demonstrations at Porton Down biological-warfare research station, in Wiltshire); and a broadening co-operation with local ecology groups. Many of these groups had developed from protests against French nuclear tests in the Pacific. Later, the newly formed Ecology Party affiliated to CND, and relations with Friends of the Earth and Greenpeace became close (Chapter 3, Val Stevens). As Taylor and Pritchard's study indicates, the environmental movement of the 1970s was a coalition in many ways analogous and related to CND in the early 1960s, and it became an important forerunner to CND's current revival. Many of the present members of the Campaign joined by way of opposition to nuclear energy, which has become part of CND's programme (Chapter 5, Howard Clark). However, there remains a section which does not favour this extension of policy (Chapter 5, John Fremlin).

From the early 1970s onward the Campaign emphasised three important points; its wisdom in doing so was born out as the years passed. It declared (1) that even the 1972 Strategic Arms Limitation Treaty (SALT-1) between Russia and America contained a dangerous weakness – while it agreed to limit the number of nuclear missiles it ignored improvements in those missiles, including the multiplication of war heads (bombs) on each missile; (2) that an urgent need was to stop the spread of nuclear weapons to an increasing number of countries; (3) that a most menacing development in the arms race was the American move to introduce a "counterforce" strategy based on a naïve belief in the possibility of a pre-emptive nuclear strike by US missiles against Soviet missiles before those missiles could be fired. Of course this policy could be applied equally by the Soviet Union; the total result was to bring the danger of nuclear war much nearer.

Sadly, these warnings have been justified. The power of nuclear weapons *has* indeed been multiplied, mainly by the increase of warheads and of their accuracy. The most obvious example is the Trident II-D5 missile carrying at least fourteen warheads each with a destructive power equal to 150,000 tons of TNT. Each Trident submarine will have the destructive power of 2,500 Hiroshima bombs, capable of being directed to 200 targets. Despite the Non-Proliferation Treaty, which came into force in March 1970, more and more countries *are* attaining the capacity to produce nuclear weapons, and the continuing arms race between the countries already owning nuclear weapons is encouraging this. And the accuracy of modern missiles *is* making more plausible a counterforce policy by which one side could in a crisis be tempted to strike first in an effort to destroy most of its opponent's missiles in their silos, thus initiating a nuclear war.

Growing fears about the accelerating speed of the nuclear arms race received a sudden jolt in the late 1970s with the appearance of the neutron bomb. The American proposal to arm NATO forces with these weapons did more than anything that had gone before to unify and activate the European anti nuclear weapons movement. Holland, West Germany, Belgium and Britain all organised energetic campaigns against the neutron bomb. The British campaign, with its widely signed petition, formed an important early stage in CND's revival.

By 1979 CND's revival had already begun, as several of the contributors to Chapter 3 show. But the public was not encouraged to notice. Writing in *New Society* in June 1979, David White noted with apparent regret:

> As the decline in CND membership shows, people have become bored with the bomb.

In fact, national membership was rising for the second year running and rose in that year alone by 30 per cent. True, there were still only about 4,000 of us: even so, we were astonished to hear a professor of sociology inform us on BBC radio soon afterwards that we were members of a non-existent organisation! "Now," said Laurie Taylor on *Stop the Week*, "there's no CND."

Since 1980 ...

The growth of the Campaign during 1980 left no room for doubt. National membership more than doubled and activity mushroomed. When you look at the political context, it's hardly surprising.

In May 1979 Mrs Thatcher had arrived at the head of a British government with a more child-like faith in nuclear deterrence than *any* of its predecessors. It was even committed to increasing "defence" spending while cutting back on almost all other public spending and to maintaining Britain's independent nuclear weapons. By December that year it had also acquiesced in NATO's plans to site new "theatre" nuclear weapons in Europe, including 160 Cruise missiles in Britain. The impotence of such a strategy was underlined a fortnight later when the West's already plentiful nuclear armoury could not prevent Russian intervention in Afghanistan.

January 1980 saw a debate on nuclear weapons in the House of Commons, during which it emerged that for ten years successive British governments had continued with a secret £1000,000,000 modernisation of her Polaris fleet – the "Chevaline" programme. (This included a Labour government publicly committed to running down Polaris.) By July, Mr Pym had announced the government's decision to buy the American Trident submarine-based missile system to replace Britain's Polaris; even then, the estimated cost was over £5,000,000,000. Meanwhile, in February, *Panorama* had exposed British civil defence planning, including the pre-recorded *Protect and Survive* films to be transmitted in the run-up to a nuclear war. The BBC was deluged with anxious and angry correspondence and the government announced that it would be putting its "Home Defence" book of the same name on sale. The earnest banality of *Protect and Survive* remains one of the most effective means of recruiting members to CND. The government seemed keen to prove they were not joking: in August, 1980 they announced that spending on such "Home Defence" would be *increased* by 20 per cent per year for the following three years.

The British sites for American Cruise missiles, Greenham Common and Molesworth, had been announced two months earlier; public confidence in their safety was hardly helped by the news, also in June, that a computer error had brought American nuclear bombers to the brink of action twice within a few days. When Ronald Reagan won the presidential election in November, alarm in Britain was further increased. Like Mrs Thatcher, he was committed to increasing arms spending: over the following year he gave the go-ahead to, among other things, the manufacture of the neutron bomb. It also emerged that 100,000 American hospital beds were on permanent standby to receive casualties from a nuclear war fought in Europe.

Nuclear warfare was no longer unthinkable, nuclear weapons were no longer simply the "ultimate deterrent". By the end of 1981, Reagan himself had said that he believed in the possibility of a "limited" nuclear war being contained in Europe; and when his Secretary of State suggested that NATO had a contingency plan to drop a *single* nuclear bomb on the Eastern bloc to demonstrate the West's determination, he promised to make enquiries to see if that was indeed part of his defence policy!

The political climate, then, was hardly reassuring. As early as April 1980 BBC Radio reported an opinion poll showing that over 40 per cent of their sample thought a nuclear war was likely *within the next 10 years*. A number of those who expected disaster tried to protect themselves individually. By that summer *New Scientist* estimated that there were already 300 firms in Britain marketing fallout shelters, radiation suits and the like. (This evidence of widespread apprehension, extending well beyond the ranks of CND supporters, was not apparent during the Campaign's earlier peak, twenty-odd years ago).

While events constantly reminded people of the imminent danger of nuclear war, a crucial additional factor began increasingly to shape the response of many. For over twenty years their leaders had looked firmly towards multilateral disarmament – and moved steadily backwards: the number of nuclear warheads deployed had risen from a few thousand to about 50,000. If you wanted to achieve anything beyond a private family fallout shelter, it seemed that multilateralism would not be enough. And there *were* signs that ordinary people could force changes: the Dutch peace movement, as Cathy Ashton (Chapter 3) explains, had led the campaign against the neutron bomb in Europe; they now seemed to be able to thwart their government's desire to accept Cruise missiles.

In Britain it was not just CND that was stirring: a whole range of groups – some old, many new – began to converge in early 1980 over their concern about nuclear weapons. *Protect and Survive* prompted Edward Thompson to write *Protest and Survive*: the pamphlet was published jointly by CND and another established group, the Bertrand Russell Peace Foundation. In turn, the Russell Foundation helped to set up the new European Nuclear Disarmament movement, END. On the anniversary of the Harrisberg accident, in March, Friends of the Earth organised what looked like being the biggest anti-nuclear demonstration of the year, with over 15,000 people in Trafalgar Square. Prominent among supporting groups was the Anti Nuclear Campaign which, as Val Stevens explains (Chapter 3), helped to link up protest against nuclear energy with protest against nuclear weapons. At the start of the year, Fenner Brockway and Philip Noel-Baker had launched the World Disarmament Campaign, aimed particularly at preparing mass petitions for the 1982 UN Special Session on disarmament. And by the end of June, the Labour Party had surprised many, and perhaps itself, by getting over 20,000 people to march against Cruise and Trident on the wettest Sunday of the summer.

Many of the vital initiatives came from local "Against the Missiles" groups. CND, a national organisation with still only four employees, did what it could to publicise them and co-ordinate support. In March 1980 simultaneous demonstrations against Cruise were held in Oxford and Cambridge: between them they mustered about 2,000 people. In July, 1,500 protesters turned up at Molesworth, only two and a half weeks after this Cruise missile site had been announced. August saw demonstrations numbering thousands of supporters at Manchester, Greenham Common and York (marching from the House Defence College).

"Protest and Survive" was adopted as the slogan for a CND march to Trafalgar Square on 26 October 1980. Could the movement keep up its momentum? In the event, it was a colossal success, with *over 80,000* at the final rally. (Bruce Kent recollects that one year earlier the Campaign had been well satisfied with an indoor meeting, 600 strong.) Even the papers were positive: 'Marchers Revive CND's Golden Years" said the *Guardian*: "CND Born Again" proclaimed the *Mail*.

Soon after this march came two significant episodes. On 5 November, Manchester City Council declared itself a "Nuclear-Free Zone" and invited other local authorities to join them. As Philip Bolsover indicates (Chapter 4), this led in less than two years to a spectacular tally of over 140 local authorities declaring themselves nuclear-free, many refusing to take part in the government's proposed Hard Rock civil-defence exercise. When the government was forced to abandon the exercise, the nuclear disarmament movement registered its most substantial victory to date. And as with so much of the movement's best work, the initiative had come more from the grassroots than from the centre: CND rightly sees one of its main roles as a clearing house and communications network for new ideas.

The other episode came on 6 November, when the *Daily Mirror* ran a shock issue, with eight pages headed "Britain and the Bomb". It included a short article by Bruce Kent, carefully balanced with one by David Owen, and an editorial clearly disowning the unilateralist view. Despite this, the *Mirror* had to ask Bruce to collect literally sackfuls of mail expressing support: clearly the public wanted to hear the Campaign's case.

1980 ended with the movement consolidating its organisation. Loose regional structures were set up or revived to allow groups from neighbouring areas to work together. The chances were that for every town or village with a CND group, there would be another represented by a group of END or ANC, by an "Against the Missiles" group or simply a Peace Group. The picture looked untidy, but relations were usually amiable: many of these diverse groups have since added "CND" to their names and now operate as CND groups, but, as Joan Ruddock explains (Chapter 4), there has been no pressure on them to do so.

The first national CND demonstration of 1981 was not until June so the regional groupings were soon put to the test. They seemed to work. In January thousands took part in a week of action on Tyneside. In March, 16,000 people demonstrated in Sheffield. Just before Easter hundreds of people tramped across the Pennines with over 10,000 finishing in Manchester. A thousand-strong British contingent joined an international Easter rally in Brussells. Simultaneous festivals and rallies were held on Tyneside and in East Anglia, in Bath, Rugby, Plymouth, Greenham Common and other centres. Bruce Kent was even whisked from Rugby to Greenham by motorbike, to speak to both!

At the beginning of June the Campaign ran a march, rally and festival on Clydeside: during much of the vital period leading up to the demonstration it looked as if it would be caught up in a 'blanket ban' on marches in the area. Despite this, 20,000 were at the final rally. Later that month 20,000 more people gathered for the Glastonbury Festival: this wasn't run *by* CND, but the organisers who had been keeping the event going biennially for the previous ten years, decided to invite CND speakers and offer all the proceeds to the Campaign. The success of the festival led to its being run for CND again in June 1982: in spite of appalling weather, the numbers doubled.

Large numbers are encouraging, of course, and occasional huge crowds compel attention — at least temporarily. But one of the greatest strengths of the Campaign of the 1980s is surely the proliferation of *small* groups of supporters who are prepared to take responsible initiatives on their own. Few of these smaller groups can have had more impact than the Women for Life on Earth. At the end of August 1981 they began a march from South Wales to

Greenham Common. After the march they didn't all go home: they started a "peace camp", squatting outside the gates of the base, occasionally blockading them. They were still there over a year later, having been moved from one owner's land to another. Some have served short terms in jail for non-violent civil disobedience, to be greeted with flowers and early morning crowds on their release. They have been the focus of large supporting demonstrations, including a colossal turn-out of 30,000 women, to embrace the base's 9 mile perimeter fence on 12 December 1982; they have spoken on radio and television. Perhaps most important, they have sparked off a chain reaction; since they began their protest many other "peace camps" have been set up, including those at Molesworth, at Fairford, at Upper Heyford, at Welford, at Burtonwood and at Bridgend (see Tony Simpson, Chapter 8). There was even one set up for a week in Porth which received a personal visit and encouragement from Michael Foot. By working in this way, non-violently, small groups have often made a deep and positive impression.

October 1981, however, brings us back to the numbers game. This time it was not just a question of British CND: within six weeks major anti-nuclear demonstrations took place all over Europe. On 10 October, well over 250,000 gathered in Bonn. On the weekend of 24/25 October there were 10,000 in Oslo, 50,000 in Paris, 50,000 in Potsdam (East Germany), 80,000 in Helsinki, at least 120,000 in Brussels and hundreds of thousands in Rome. And, of course, there was a turnout variously estimated at 150,000 to over 250,000 in London. Whatever the precise figure, this was without question the largest British CND demonstration *ever*. In both size and mood it finally moved us beyond the shadow of the "good old days" of CND. Huge and purposeful, good-humoured and trouble-free, it represented a massive achievement on the part of the thousands of groups who were there, the hundreds of volunteer helpers and, most of all perhaps, the handful of CND's dozen full-time staff who organised it. The press was hardly able to fault the event and had to concede the very wide spectrum of support they found. However, the *Sunday Express* managed to complain that the sheer numbers present "caused traffic chaos throughout London ... tying up hundreds of uniformed policemen".

In the book *Nukespeak: the Media and the Bomb*, Ian Connell's article makes the interesting suggestion that 24 October 1981 represented a sort of watershed in media coverage of CND and the nuclear issue. Certainly the immediate follow-up supports this view with Bruce Kent being given an extended discussion with FO minister. Douglas Hird, on Radio 4's *The World this Weekend* the next day, and Monday's *Thought for the Day* being devoted to Rev Richard Sims's glowing account of what it felt like to take part. Even the American government agreed that the October demonstrations should be taken seriously: Reagan admitted to having spent a session discussing them with his advisers. His "Zero Option", however superficial as an offer to the

Russians, represented a salutary change in tone.

By way of a sting in the tail came the 21 November Amsterdam demo where 500,000 (one-thirtieth of the entire Dutch population) came out to oppose nuclear weapons.

In Britain, 1982 saw further consolidation of CND's growth. National membership was up again, about 50,000 by November and local group membership may have climbed to ten times that figure. The Campaign now employs over two dozen full-time staff, with an increasing proportion working in the regions and directly responsible to one of CND's 16 regional councils. *Sanity*, CND's paper, returned to monthly publication in September 1982 for the first time since 1971. Its circulation when first relaunched in this way was over 40,000. Among CND's recent successful pamphlets, *Questions and Answers* by Frank Allaun and *Atoms for War* by Howard Clark have circulated 30,000 and 25,000 copies respectively. CND sales, which of course deals also with posters, badges, etc, and relevant books from other publishers, had a turnover of £200,000 in 1981. In the same period CND had (excluding sales) an overall income and expenditure of £400,000.

The Campaign voted at the end of 1981 to enlarge its National Council to include five delegates from each region as well as the chairperson, vice chairperson, treasurer and twenty other directly elected members. There is also a National Council place for each of CND's specialist sections, including Youth, Christian, Trade-Union, Student, Liberal, Labour and Green CND.

As well as these sections there is an endless list of "parallel groups" which have been started up independently. These include Scientists Against Nuclear Arms, the Medical Campaign Against Nuclear Weapons, Journalists Against Nuclear Extermination, Teachers for Peace, Families Against the Bomb, Women Oppose the Nuclear Threat, Tories Against Cruise and Trident (TACT) and even, recently, Babies Against the Bomb! Most of these are affiliated to national CND as are over 1,000 organisations. A large number of Trades Unions are affiliated, including the T&GWU, NALGO, NUPE, ASTMS and others representing about six million members in all. One union, the National Association for Teachers in Further and Higher Education, recently amended its own constitution to allow it to affiliate.

There is a similar wide range of church groups associated with the Campaign. An important event in autumn, 1982, was the publication of a report by a Church of England working party which called for Britain to abandon nuclear weapons. At about the same time a London Weekend Television survey showed that 40 per cent of Church of England clergy believed Britain should scrap her nuclear "deterrent".

Much of 1982's activity has been at the crucially important local level. Local CND groups have organised demonstrations, meetings, festivals, etc, attracting hundreds, even sometimes thousands of supporters. MPs have received petitions from local groups with the signatures of many thousands of their constituents. Literature stalls have been kept going month in, month out. During the Easter "Peace Week", *Sanity* reported over thirty major demonstrations across the country.

Likewise, support for parallel groups has been encouraged. In March about 6,000 people spent a day at Greenham Common, in support of the Women's Peace Camp. Thousands joined the mass lobby of Parliament, organised in May by Families Against the Bomb.

There have been national CND activities as well. On 6 June 1982 came CND's main mass demonstration for the year, timed for the eve of Reagan's visit to Britain. As it happened, it also coincided with the tail end of the Falklands War; this had distracted many people's attention from the longer term problems of nuclear weapons, and worked others up into an infantile state of jingoism. There could hardly have been a more difficult moment for the Campaign to follow up the success of 24 October 1981. In the event, the turnout was astonishing: estimates varied from 115,000 (lowest police figure) to 250,000. Though marginally down on the colossal October figure, it was still CND's second biggest demo *ever*.

More recently has come the nationally co-ordinated "Operation Hard Luck". Designed to spell out the effects of a nuclear war right across Britain, it was similar in conception to the Campaign's "Fallex" exercise nineteen years earlier. But the contrasts could hardly be sharper. Fallex was a frustrating uphill struggle by a movement in decline, in the teeth of official hostility and public apathy. Hard Luck came in the wake of the Campaign's triumph in getting the Government to abandon Hard Rock; many local authorities co-operated even to the point of opening their emergency bunkers to public view; and the public, whether they were currently listening to CND or Mrs Thatcher, or simply watching TV, could hardly be oblivious of the nuclear weapons issue.

In fact, Hard Rock is not the *only* nuclear plan the government have abandoned recently. Another is the projected development of Trident servicing facilities at Coulport, Scotland: the plan is now for the Independent British Nuclear Virility Symbol of the 1990s to be dependent on American servicing, as well as supply. The overwhelming local hostility towards Trident on Clydeside must, by now, be clear to the government since they have just lost a parliamentary seat there.

These victories are a useful start. So too is the improved flow of information about the effects of nuclear war. The BBC TV documentary *QED: Guide to Armageddon* marks another breakthrough: twenty years ago it could hardly have been made, let alone shown.

Opinion polls are encouraging too. A recent *Guardian* Marplan poll showed an 8 per cent increase in support for Britain abandoning nuclear weapons in the seventeen months up to September 1982. In Scotland, a *Glasgow Herald* poll already showed majority support for CND by December 1981.

By 1982, the Labour Party had committed itself at three successive conferences to opposing British nuclear weapons and all nuclear bases in Britain. The Liberal Party was now opposed to Cruise missiles and many aspects of Britain's nuclear policy, though David Steel seemed intent on flouting the party's wishes on this issue. The Nationalist, Ecology and Communist parties all supported CND. Even the SDP opposed the British plan to buy Trident.

The Campaign has always been under-represented in Parliament and this is still so. An *approximate* figure for MPs supporting CND would be 125. This assumes the support of the two Welsh Nationalists, at least one Scots Nationalist, two Liberals, three others and nearly 120 Labout MPs who are members of Parliamentary Labour CND.

If this quick glance at CND's history can teach us anything it is surely that we should *not* allow the Campaign to submerge its identity in any single party. We have an increasing number of members right across the conventional political spectrum (including some Conservatives). It's up to the candidates to convince us that they really are against nuclear weapons. It's up to us to make sure that more and more ordinary people *demand* that they are.

There is, as they say, no alternative!

John Minnion
Philip Bolsover
December 1982

CHAPTER ONE
Aldermaston and the Early Years

An account by **Mervyn Jones** of the first Aldermaston March is supplemented by **John Brunner**'s recollections of how groups of musicians organised support. **Jo Richardson** remembers the experience of laying on food and drink for the next three Aldermastons. **April Carter** describes the work of the Direct Action Committee during its four years from 1957. Finally, **Janey** and **Norman Buchan** sketch in some of the distinctive elements and episodes that characterised the movement in Scotland during those early years.

Aldermaston 1958
Mervyn Jones

CND was launched in 1958, as it was to be relaunched in 1980, on a wave of enthusiasm that took the planners by surprise. It seemed wildly optimistic to take the Central Hall for the inaugural meeting on a Monday night in February, especially as small ads in papers like the *New Statesman* and *Peace News* were the only publicity. But 5,000 people came along and the speakers had to shuttle to four overflow meetings. Within a few weeks, thousands joined groups up and down the country.

What were we going to do? The word went round: "March to Aldermaston at Easter." This project wasn't the brainchild of CND, but of the Direct Action Committee against Nuclear War, formed some months earlier. (CND organisation of the march, with Peggy Duff in charge and the big Co-op caravan as mobile headquarters, dates from 1959.) Someone said to me: "There's this extraordinary girl called Pat Arrowsmith."

It seemed pretty wild, too. Several of the CND founding fathers had envisaged a pressure-group working through lobbying and deputations, not a mass movement. The accepted idea of a march was Marble Arch to Trafalgar Square, not a distance of 45 miles. Many people said that it was crazy to march *away* from London. Indeed, the first march to Aldermaston was to be the last until 1972; from 1959, the direction was reversed. The original black-and-white banner was carried year after year, with the word "from" sewn over 1958's "to".

Mainly through Peggy's urging, CND decided to back the march and worked harmoniously with Direct Action. I was then on the staff of *Tribune*, and I often walked over to CND's first office in a courtyard off Fleet Street.

The first Aldermaston march, 1958. (*Photo:* Henry Grant.)

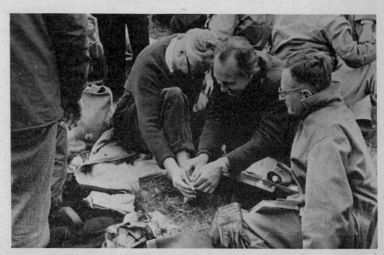

Frank Allaun, MP, on the 1958 London to Aldermaston march. (*Photo:* courtesy of Frank Allaun.)

You could hardly get up the stairs for the throng of young people who came to make placards or collect bundles of leaflets. Clearly, the march was going to start off with a bang. The question was, how many people would get beyond the suburbs?

We showed up in Trafalgar Square at eleven o'clock on Good Friday morning. Quite a nice sunny day, though far from warm. Quite a good crowd, though short of filling the Square. Canon Collins and others made speeches. We set off, heading for the lunch stop at the Albert Memorial. A distinction was obvious: between those equippped with anoraks and rucksacks, who intended to go all the way, and those – much more numerous – who were in the respectable urban clothes of the period and limiting themselves to the first stage. The target for the day was Turnham Green, and it was easy to get home from there by tube. Personally, as I'd brought my five-year-old son, I didn't even go that far.

On Saturday morning, I made my way to Turnham Green to march to Slough. The weather had abruptly changed and was appalling, with bitter cold and incessant rain. The dreariness of the Great West Road, with cars splashing the column of marchers, didn't help either. After a time, we realised that it wasn't raining any more – it was snowing, the first Easter snow for a century. We made a stop at the Peggy Bedford Inn, at Cranford. The plastic bag hadn't yet been invented and our sandwiches were wrapped in paper, so they were soaked. The landlord, bless him, provided free soup.

It hadn't occurred to anybody that the CND big-shots were expected to do any marching; those pictures of the Canon in his cassock, Michael Foot with his stick and his dog, and Jacquetta Hawkes in her splendid red hat were taken in subsequent years. The only "name" that Saturday, if I remember rightly, was Frank Allaun. The march, therefore, had a pleasantly amateurish flavour, and hardly anybody was over 25 years old. But we were few, sadly few. At the Peggy Bedford I counted 300, and some dropped out or hitched lifts during the miserable afternoon. There was a serious question of whether the march was going to peter out.

As we trudged into Slough, people living along the road were bemused but sympathetic. A man dashed out of his house and said: "You might like to know that Cambridge won by three lengths." A woman went into a shop, bought a box of toffees, and handed them out. True, a man on the steps of the Conservative Association shouted: "Go back to Moscow!" – but a marcher instantly replied: "Go back to Torrington!" (where the Tories had lost a by-election) and that got a laugh. The Methodist minister opened his church at an hour's notice and miraculously found tea and biscuits for everybody.

One of the marchers was a girl, slightly built and five-foot nothing tall, holding one pole of a heavy banner. A nail from one shoe gave her a blister and she limped from Maidenhead on. At Slough, she fell asleep during the welcoming speech from the local MP, Fenner Brockway. I reckoned she'd done her bit.

I took a day off and didn't march the Sunday stretch, from Slough to Reading. On Monday, the gods relented and it was fine again. The *Sunday Express* had run a smear story about "celebrities" who endorsed the march and stayed at home, there had been some urgent phoning, and for the final day there was a good turnout of the kind that led to Aldermaston being called "the Ascot of the Left". I shared the picnic lunch at Burghfield with Kenneth Tynan, Doris Lessing and Christopher Logue. The Vicar had produced a leaflet telling us that nuclear war might be the divine will and it was sinful to question it. I wish I'd kept it; it was a classic of its kind.

Nearing Aldermaston, the lush farming landscape changed to a heathland of gorse and pines, deserted and – all things considered – fairly sinister. In marshy pools, according to Logue, lurked creatures mutated by radiation. "Frogs as big as Volkswagens", he declaimed. None of us had seen the place where the bombs were made, and we peered at it with a sense of awe as we marched along the perimeter fence. Mysterious pipes led in all directions; the buildings were sinister just because of their apparent attractiveness and innocence. I described it as a cross between an oil refinery and a comprehensive school.

But the march had become enormous! Well – enormous by the expectations of 1958; actually the count was 4,000. At a crossroads, we were joined by a healthy contingent from Wessex. Looking back from a hill, we saw the column stretching as far as the road was visible. Friends shouted to each other in delight; cameras clicked. After the doubts, after the crossed fingers, our venture was a success. We had truly started something.

That girl – the girl with the blister – was still there, marching barefoot now and carrying her shoes. She made one whispered complaint during the speeches: "I wish they'd stop telling us how splendid we are." I wrote about her in my report in *Tribune*, and later I put her in a novel, but I don't know who she is because she ticked me off for trying to personalise the Campaign and wouldn't tell me her name. I wonder where she is now.

Music on the March
John Brunner

At the first meeting of CND in February 1958, members of the Direct Action Committee were handing out leaflets announcing the Easter march from London to AWRE Aldermaston.

Marjorie and I, who before we met had been going to separate skiffle clubs, thought what a good idea it would be if we could persuade some of our musical friends not merely to join in, but also to publicise it by going ahead to sing and play on street-corners, at stations, in pubs, and so forth.

Very shortly we discovered we weren't the only people to have had such an inspiration. Eric Winter, editor of *Sing* – Dr John Hasted – Betty and Fred (now better known as Karl) Dallas – Rita and John ("The Broadsheet King") Foreman – John Holley – Ray and Wendy Edwards and other members of the London Youth Choir ... all of a sudden literally scores of people were getting involved, some of whom had already composed and performed notable anti-Bomb songs, such as the Dallases' powerful "Doomsday Blues".

Most of us got together at the Princess Louise in Holborn, a famous skiffle venue, and agreed that what we most needed was a song specially written for the march. I had one in draft, but it wasn't very singable and I needed a tune for it: not one to which everybody already knew the words, yet easy to learn, and with a good marchable beat. It was John Hasted who proposed using "Miner's Lifeguard", previously a gospel hymn called "Life is like a Mountain Railway". Everybody around the table helped to recast my first verse into a chorus, and then I took the text away and revised the rest to fit the tune. Result: "The H-Bombs' Thunder", later to be known as "the National Anthem of the British Peace Movement".

Then, shortly before Easter, we held a meeting at Marjorie's flat in Swiss Cottage, which included other people such as singer Joe Moss and Maltese clarinetist Oreste Doneo, and got ourselves organised into groups and worked out a rough schedule. We agreed that we would operate in stages, going ahead of the march to the next town it would reach to attract attention with the music and hand out publicity material explaining how important a matter we were demonstrating for.

The DAC was not entirely happy with the wide range of support their venture was receiving, and insisted on censoring the songs we planned to use; indeed the group we worked with had a member of DAC assigned to it – unkindly nicknamed "The Gauleiter" – to ensure we remained ideologically pure ...

But this internal policing was largely in vain, because the attendance, especially on the final day, was so much greater than expected. Moreover, we were far from the only musical contributors. At one time or another we ran across several jazzbands, *ad hoc*, amateur and professional: Ken Colyer's Omega Brass Band turned out on the first day. The Youth Choir did incredible service, particularly during the snowstorm of Saturday morning, and John Foreman dropped in and out of the march with song-sheets, teaching enough people the tunes to keep them singing and then moving on.

Our reception was mixed. We have pictures of ourselves singing to an empty station forecourt in Reading, and in a number of pubs we were harshly challenged by the customers. I remember above all a woman with a raucous voice to whom I dearly wanted to say: "Madam, our ambition is to live to be your age" – for she was so obviously disguising it. But we were pledged to avoid even verbal violence …

On the other hand, a surprising and gratifying number of passers-by stopped to listen, read our leaflets, and even applauded us. A good many from Reading decided to join the final rally in Falcon Field … where, for me, everything was made worthwhile by a comment from John Holley: the soaking, the sore feet, the hoarseness, everything.

Little by little the song which kept being repeated turned out to be "The H-Bombs' Thunder". Like the ND symbol, it had caught people's fancy, and by Monday it was being sung to a weird variety of tunes. And, as we were waiting to enter the field, opposite the forbidding fence of AWRE, John told me, "That's it – that's the one. Your song says it all."

I felt about eight feet tall.

Not on that march, but a later one, we shipped an entire steel band to Aldermaston, and the corpus of songs multiplied and we eventually made records of them like "Songs from Aldermaston" by the London Youth Choir: despite which I'm advised that even now, if they want to play "The H-Bombs Thunder", people in the BBC have to apply to higher authority for special permission.

Talk about great oaks from little acorns, though!

Tea for 20,000
Jo Richardson

Imagine being faced with the task of providing hot drinks and snacks at least three times a day for three and a half days, and each time at a different spot. And imagine trying to organise this from scratch with little money, no equipment, no form of transport – and, most important, no idea of how many people to cater for. (In fact we started out at 10,000 and finished at around 20,000.) This was what faced me and a small band of helpers on the 1959 Aldermaston March.

A march from Aldermaston to London had never been undertaken before. Peggy Duff and the CND Committee had no idea what to expect in terms of numbers, and of course with an operation like that – a trek beginning on Good Friday morning and continuing until we reached Trafalgar Square on Easter Monday – no one could calculate who would need overnight accommodation in schools or would go home and return next day, and how many would bring their own food and drink. The accommodation wasn't my problem: the feeding of the marchers was.

As I sat down to try and calculate how much food we would need (no chance over a Bank Holiday weekend of finding reserve supplies), what equipment we must get hold of and how all of it could be transported, the job seemed impossible. I made list after list of suggested snacks and quantities, revising them over the weeks as more information began to trickle through. I rang different suppliers for quotes and for ideas, though bearing in mind all along that I wanted to use the Co-op if possible.

I drove over the route several times, sometimes with others involved in this and other tasks, to check out the stopping points for water supplies and space for parking for our vehicles and putting out our trestle tables; finally I took the plunge and ordered the supplies.

As with all undertakings of this sort, volunteers began to emerge who could provide practical help.

The first and most practical helper was Bert Harrington, who owned and ran a café in Tunbridge Wells. Bert volunteered not only himself and his expertise, but all the urns and other equipment needed for making hot drinks. (We used hired field-kitchens to boil the water.)

Bert was the only professional amongst the rest of us amateurs, and what a tower of strength he was. He knew exactly how long the water took to boil, and what quantities of tea we needed, and when he wasn't supervising that end of it he helped out with other tasks. The other principal helpers were Peggy Solomons, Secretary of Slough CLP, Ian Mikardo, Joy Mostyn, and Jimpy Mendham – a young man who brought along a van, and who wore a woolly hat which he never took off. He was constantly cheerful and impish. We gradually acquired transport (as I recall we only had to hire one large lorry – the rest was contributed) and trestle tables, and finally, we packed everything up and set off for Aldermaston around dawn on Good Friday.

That day was our dummy run. That was the day we discovered in really practical terms what we had packed in the wrong order (the tea equipment was buried behind carton after carton of fruit pies, meat pies, sausage rolls, bread rolls, soft drinks, biscuits and chocolate); and we realised what we had forgotten to bring, how many more helpers we needed and so on. That was the day we took so long repacking everything at one stop that the march was well on the way to the next halt: we couldn't get round them with our eight vehicles, and had to make a desperate dash round the lanes of Berkshire in order to arrive before the March and get the water boiling and the food laid out. That was the day it dawned on us that charging 7d for a Lyons individual fruit pie meant giving 5d change for a shilling, that counting it out took time and anyway we didn't have enough coppers!

After our first mistakes, things went more smoothly. We got our logistics right and sent off most of our vehicles before the march left its stopping place. The marchers themselves knew what to expect and had their money ready –

all of them always cheerful, friendly and good-humoured. Problems still arose of course. Rain and wind are not the easiest of elements to cope with when you're boiling up water, but Bert Harrington became expert in finding the most sheltered spots to get the tea going. The worst difficulties were at Reading, when the local Tory Council would not provide schools or any other facilities for the marchers overnight, with the result that they had to sleep under canvas in a quagmire of mud.

We catered for the Easter Marches for two more years – once again from Aldermaston, and one in which half the march came from Aldermaston and the other half from Weathersfield, which meant recruiting more people to help and tackling a new route.

But it worked out all right. We got more ambitious about food too. We supplied soup, which by the third day became unrecognisable as anything but a brownish liquid – but it was hot and wet and the marchers continued to be cheerful! We provided hard boiled eggs; and while marchers settled down for the night in schools and halls, we sat around our urns boiling hundreds of eggs for their breakfasts.

Ian Mikardo reckons he carried two tons of water over one weekend. Certainly all of us used muscles we didn't know we had, and became ingenious at improvising for what we hadn't got. But everyone was there to show their opposition to the Bomb – organisers, caterers, drivers, and above all marchers. That's why there really were no cross words and no problems that couldn't eventually be solved, in that marvellous spirit of comradeship which is my abiding memory of those Easter Marches.

Direct Action Against Nuclear War
April Carter

The Direct Action Committee arose out of a protest against the testing of the first British H-Bomb at Christmas Island in 1957. An ad hoc committee organised support for the attempt by Quaker Harold Steele to sail from Japan into the nuclear testing area. Harold Steele was not able to reach the testing zone, but the group who had backed his protest decided to continue the campaign in Britain. The principles which underlay the plan to enter the testing zone – belief in the need for non-violent action directed against the weapons and bases designed for nuclear warfare, the need for personal commitment, and reliance on popular protest rather than on working through the established political process – characterised the activities of the Direct Action Committee during its existence from 1957-61.

The first action initiated by this Committee was a march from London to Aldermaston, where research on nuclear weapons took place. It was planned for the four days of Easter 1958. The march was organised with the active help of the Labour H-Bomb Committee and the Universities and Left Review Club; and it gained impetus from the newly formed Campaign for Nuclear Disarmament, which gave the march its blessing. In later years CND ran the Aldermaston March as its own major symbolic event, while the much smaller, and more radical, DAC turned its attention to other forms of campaigning.

The DAC was internationalist in its theory, hoping for the development of popular protest against government nuclear policies in the United States and, despite the obvious problems, in the USSR. It therefore offered co-operation to the American Committee for Non-Violent Action in organising the European section of the San Francisco to Moscow March of 1960-61. The DAC took the initiative when France proclaimed its intention of joining the nuclear club, and of testing its first atomic bombs in the Sahara desert in 1960. The French left was largely preoccupied with opposing the Algerian War and was hampered by the new Gaullist régime, but some French citizens supported the DAC idea of an international protest team which aimed to enter the Sahara testing area. The proposal received active support from the American CNVA; and many Africans, who were outraged by the use of their continent for nuclear testing, volunteered to join the team. Michael Scott, then well known in Africa for his work at the United Nations on behalf of the Hereros of South-West Africa, was one of the DAC members of the team, which was given full backing by the newly independent government of Ghana. The team made several unsuccessful attempts to get past the French military controlling the route to the Sahara testing site; although the protest remained purely symbolic, it did provide a focus for widespread protest and publicity in Africa against the French tests.

At home the DAC was best known for its obstruction at nuclear bases. The first major civil disobedience demonstrations took place in December, 1958, at the site of one of the Thor missile bases being built then in Norfolk. The first time demonstrators walked onto the site and tried to stop work on the Swaffham base, they were met with minor violence. Two weeks later DAC supporters returned, blocked the entrance, and were arrested; thirty spent a week in prison over Christmas.

Both protests received extensive and quite favourable publicity, and as a result the CND Executive came under pressure to give greater support to the DAC. A year later the CND organised a sympathy march outside the Harrington Thor base, while 80 DAC supporters committed civil disobedience; six members of the DAC itself were already in prison, bound over for two months for refusing to call off the demonstration.

The final protest organised by the Committee was an attempt to board a Proteus depot ship and block the pier at Holy Loch in the summer of 1961. This action took place at the end of a march from London to Holy Loch, and

DAC sit-down at the gates of the Polaris base, Holy Loch, 1961.

Bertrand Russell, Hugh McDiarmid smoking his pipe, with other demonstrators in a Committee of 100 sit-down outside the Ministry of Defence, February 1961. (*Photo:* Henry Grant.)

was strongly supported by Labour, trade-union and CND groups in the Glasgow area, who had mobilised an impressive local campaign against the use of Holy Loch by American nuclear missile submarines.

The Holy Loch protest came the closest to achieving what the DAC had hoped for in earlier campaigns: civil disobedience occurring as one element in a movement of local opposition to nuclear bases. In Scotland the opposition had been generated by the militant left-wing traditions and national consciousness of Clydeside. In the less promising areas of East Anglia and the Midlands, civil disobedience at missile bases had been preceded by weeks of local campaigning by the DAC, including numerous meetings with trade-union branches, in the hope of persuading unionists to strike or black the bases: it was difficult to get them to translate sympathy into action.

The DAC moved from its initial position, adopted at a nine-week picket of Aldermaston in summer 1958, of appealing to workers on the basis of individual conscientious objection: the later aim was to achieve collective trade-union protests and proposals for peaceful alternatives. This approach was pursued, with some degree of success, in a number of towns where industry was involved in making parts for missiles and bombers, for example, during 1959 in Stevenage, where Blue Streak was being manufactured. During the summer of 1960 there was a four-pronged campaign in Bristol, Manchester, Weybridge and Slough to demonstrate the ramifications of nuclear arms manufacture in British industry and stimulate industrial action.

In 1961, after the Committee of 100 had been launched, with the support of DAC members, it was agreed to dissolve the DAC in the hope that its ideas would be taken up on a larger scale.*

The Campaign in Scotland: singing into protest
Janey and Norman Buchan

What gave the Campaign in Scotland its strength as well as its particularity was, of course, the coming of Polaris to the Clyde. What had been a terrifying abstraction was now only too real, visible, menacing. We had a particular target which was of immediate and direct relevance. From a very early stage, therefore, it was apparent to us that the mobilisation of opinion in Scotland was more widely based; more representative of the people in general, and therefore, in a word, more working class in character than the early days of CND elsewhere in Britain. In one sense the mix was the same – trade-union activists, academics, intellectuals – but the balance was different. And this was what gave strength and particular excitement and urgency to the struggle on the Clyde. One's first sight of the sinister black hull of a nuclear submarine slowly moving up the estuary is not only the immediate revelation of an

* A brief account of the Committee of 100 is given in the introduction, pp. 20-22.

obscenity but an enormous stimulant to action.

We knew the target. The enemy was with us. It made concrete all our theories. We had picked on Aldermaston as a symbol. But Polaris had picked on us.

We were blessed with one or two organisers of genius. Brian Smith built around him a vigorous and imaginative group of students. Two things particularly we remember. One was in pursuance of Brian's aim to make the CND symbol known and familiar "within the year".

On one early morning exercise – at about 5 a.m. – Brian got his happy team to place the black CND poster behind one of the newspaper bill hoardings at nearly a thousand shops in Glasgow. Many of them stayed up for weeks. On another occasion he succeeded in the "impossible", getting two of the big Clyde ferries to mark time in mid-stream, to allow the ferry carrying our van with anti-Polaris posters to cross the Clyde first and be there dishing out the posters as the thousands landed.

From a very early stage we had won full support from the Labour Party, Trades Council and the STUC. That seems simple now – not so easy then. And it was they who were largely responsible for securing the biggest post-war demonstration in Glasgow till then, at the start of the 1960's. Incidentally, that was the demonstration that produced the sectarian slogan to end all sectarian slogans. Just as we were turning round the corner of Sauchiehall Street two grim stalwarts of the *Socialist Party of Great Britain* were standing heralding the march with a huge banner and slogan which read: "This demonstration is useless – You must first destroy capitalism".

It was this too that led to the famous Gaitskell incident at the 1962 May Day rally in Queen's Park. The triumvirate of organisers – the Labour Party, Cooperatives and Trades Council – having first invited Gaitskell to be the speaker had then chosen the theme as "Anti-Polaris". So we had the bizarre spectacle of a May Day awash with Ban Polaris posters and a huge banner with the same slogan on the platform behind Hugh Gaitskell, who was bitterly opposed to CND. The ruction that ensued was good natured, but enough to have our constituency party facing disbandment for the next seventy-two hours … but that is another story.

We were very early struck by the difference of tone between the London and Clyde marches. And nowhere is this better illustrated than in the songs they sang. At Aldermaston the songs were hymn-like and aspirational. On the Clyde they were popular, based on street songs, cheeky and irreverent and cocking a snook. Incidents rather than abstractions were their inspiration.

With the first involvement of direct-action methods, the songs poured out. Morris Blythman and Hamish Henderson built a group of Polaris singers and song writers, building on the folk song revival flourishing at that time. Not for them the noble abstractions of "Family of Man" or "The H-Bombs'

Thunder".

There was the canoe episode when the Polaris ship, under its Commander, Lanning, first arrived at the Holy Loch in 1961. Marchers had set off from the Aldermaston March carrying their own canoes. The fleet was augmented by a local flotilla – and the Glasgow Eskimos were born. To the tune of "Marching Through Georgia" – better known in Glasgow as "The Derry Boys":

> Up the Clyde cam' Lanning, a super duper Yank,
> But doon a dam sight quicker when we drapped him doon the stank.
> Up tae yer knees in sludge and sewage fairly stops yer swank –
> We are the Glasgow Eskimos ...

(And, for the uninitiated, "stank" means drain).

Similarly the great "Ding Dong Dollar" came from this early period. This was the riposte to the claims of the government – and the Tory Town Council of Dunoon – that the coming of the Polaris base would add to the prosperity of the area. The tune was "Coming round the Mountain":

> Oh, the Yanks have jist drapped anchor at Dunoon,
> And they've got a civic welcome frae the toon,
> As they came up the measured mile,
> Bonny Mary o' Argyle
> Wis wearing spangled drawers below her goon.
> *Chorus*: Oh, ye cannae spend a dollar when ye're deid,
> Naw, ye cannae spend a dollar when ye're deid,
> Singing Ding Dong Dollar, everybody holler,
> Ye cannae spend a dollar when ye're deid.

But if the fun was there, it was there to give confidence and create elan, and, by heaven, we needed it as the Clyde estuary grew into the most horrifying nuclear base in Western Europe. First, the Holy Loch, then Faslane, then an entire mountain excavated for nuclear storage in Glen Douglas alongside Loch Lomond. So the campaign equally had to expand. Tens of thousands participated in the demonstrations. Many, many hundreds sat down at Ardnadam in silent protest – and sang on their way into overnight imprisonment in the halls that were pressed into use at Dunoon to contain them.

There were less theoretical disputes here between the direct action campaigners and the others than occurred elsewhere. Each did their own thing and respected the other, for the work was complementary.

Continuity was given throughout the period by, among others, the Chairman of CND in Scotland, Keith Bovey. And later, when, as elsewhere, the movement seemed to have faltered and faded, Ian Davison kept it alive, and better, as secretary, until the revival again in the last few years.

Always it managed to keep its contacts and its broad and popular basis. We see this resurrecting itself again in the action of local authorities, like Dunbartonshire, refusing to accept further expansion of the base, and Strathclyde Region, along with others, refusing to participate in the illusion of the Hard Rock exercise.

"Our een are on the target," we sang in 1962. And enough of the early campaigners have kept their eyes sufficiently on the target ever since, to lay the basis for the recent revival of the anti-nuclear struggle.

The old theme song is still sung –

Tell the Yanks tae drap it doon the stank,
For we dinnae want Polaris.

CHAPTER TWO
Problems of the 1960s

Though CND achieved some major successes in the early 1960s, by the end of the decade we had lost ground. Contributors to this chapter were asked to consider some of the main problems. **Frank Allaun**, while giving an overview of this difficult decade, pays particular attention to the setbacks for CND's Labour Party supporters. **Richard Gott** focuses on the tension between wings of the movement – particularly between those who wanted to develop a "grassroots" Campaign and those who sought to refine CND's thinking on nuclear strategy. **Nigel Young** discusses the impact of the 1962 Cuban crisis, and compares this with other factors that made the going difficult. **John Petherbridge** recalls the particular episodes of 1963, when British supporters became involved with the Greek anti-nuclear movement. Finally, **Dick Nettleton** draws some lessons for the future, including a warning against being too preoccupied with the past!

In with a bang, out …
Frank Allaun

The Sixties were a bad decade for CND. They came in with a bang and went out with almost nothing. In fact many observers thought the movement was finished, never suspecting the enormous growth that was to take place ten years later.

In 1960, Labour went unilateral. In the spring and summer of that year, one after the other, the big unions, which, in my view rightly, have a decisive influence on Labour Party policy, took the CND line. (Even the General and Municipal Workers' Union, which was regarded as a right-wing organisation, had gone unilateralist in 1959, but the leaders had promptly recalled the conference to reverse the decision.)

It was the leftward swing in the Transport and General Workers' Union which had started the ball rolling several years earlier, with other unions following its example. Among the Constituency Labour Parties there was never any doubt where they stood.

As a result, in October 1960 the Party conference swung behind the anti nuclear weapon line. Hugh Gaitskell, the Party leader, made his famous speech to say he would "fight, fight and fight again" to save the Party. And he did. Aided by Bill Rogers (now one of the SDP Gang of Four) and his Campaign for Democratic Socialism, and by the leaders of several of the big and more backward unions, the 1961 annual conference defeated the unilateralist policy.

Many CND-ers resolved to have nothing to do with political parties, though many of us pointed out that only government could achieve unilateral nuclear disarmament, and, in British terms, that meant either a Conservative or Labour government.

If the determination of the disarmers in the Labour Party and unions had been equal to that of their opponents, and if they had had the mass backing which they have today, I do not believe the 1961 vote would have been lost. Then our history would have been different.

Nevertheless the struggle, though limited, went on. The Cuban crisis took place in 1962, when millions of people went to bed one night wondering if they and their children would be involved in the holocaust before the morning. Both Kennedy and Krushchev learnt from the terrifying experience and began to think of co-existence.

Nuclear weapons tests continued. In Parliament, Labour MPs pressed each month for the latest figures showing the steadily growing amount of Strontium 90 from the tests found in the bones of children dying under one year of age. Cuba plus Strontium 90 accounted for the Partial Test Ban Treaty signed in 1963: America, Russia and Britain henceforth conducted their tests underground.

Ironically, it was the success of this treaty — one of the very few successes of multilateral disarmament — which did more than anything else to undermine CND. Some members of the movement sat back thinking the job had been done, when clearly it had not.

Adding to our wounds was the conduct of Harold Wilson's government, elected in 1964 and re-elected in 1966. He carried on the Conservative administration's nuclear weapons programme almost without alteration.

The Easter marches had started as early as 1958; then some of us had argued that if fifty men and women did the four-day march it would have justified itself. Never in our wildest dreams did we imagine that the CND symbol would become known throughout the world, or that the marches would continue in other countries, notably West Germany, even after the impetus had been lost in Britain. (Incidentally, I felt that the success of the original marches was helped by a defeat of the conception of some good friends who wanted them to aim at arms workers giving up their jobs. The other side argued that this would be a futile task and that the main job was to win support from the people, particularly in the Labour and trade-union movement, for forcing the government to end its nuclear war plans. I am sure the latter view was — and is — right.)

Through the 1960s the marches continued, but the movement split. The main division was between those who wanted Direct Action and those who believed in the movement growing in other ways. On the marches there were some fringe groups who seemed to me much more intent on disrupting and smashing the demonstrations than on winning nuclear disarmament. Having nationally lost its impact, the movement turned to vent its wrath on internal

Setting off from Aldermaston, 1967. The tractor, representing agricultural protests against nuclear bases in the countryside, was eventually driven into Trafalgar Square for the Easter demonstration. (*Photo:* Graham Keen.)

battles. It looked as if CND was finished. Some brave and determined men, like Dick Nettleton, continued to struggle – but it seemed to be the death throes.

Most of the activists switched to another struggle – to end the war in Vietnam. The atrocities, the massive scale, the injustice, the brutal reaction of the American government, shocked hundreds of thousands in every country in Europe – not to mention millions in the States – into massive demonstrations. CND declined further in public interest and support.

Few could have anticipated the fantastic revival due for the beginning of the Eighties, when a public opinion poll could show 63 per cent against the Trident and only 23 per cent for it, when quarter of a million could march on Hyde Park on 24 October 1981, and when even bigger demonstrations were to take place throughout Europe.

As one who has been in the anti-war struggle since leaving school, I say this is the greatest peace movement in history. I have never known in my lifetime such a massive support for the struggle against war. The reason is clear: it is because millions of people realise how near the brink we are.

The difficult years
Richard Gott

At the end of 1961, the CND movement as a whole, after some four years of multifaceted campaigning, was in difficulty as to its future strategy. The aim of the founding fathers to have a short campaign and a speedy victory had not been met. The attempt to carry the Labour Party had been a failure. The efforts of the Committee of 100 to supplement conventional campaigning methods with mass direct action had suffered from a lack of troops. It was a major crisis – though not exactly perceived as such at the time – for there was no agreement on the way forward.

No single strategy would appeal to all wings of the movement, so CND began to accept a whole range of diverse initiatives. Inevitably this produced some strains. CND supporters of the Labour Party, for example, were extremely opposed to those who advocated putting up independent anti-Bomb candidates. (INDEC, the Independent Nuclear Disarmament Election Committee, fielded one candidate, Michael Craft, who, in the general election in 1964, got more than 1,000 votes.) The Labour CNDers often looked more sympathetically on another (in some ways more revolutionary or utopian) strand in CND thinking which was to go for "the grassroots". "A movement has grown up which is not a political party", wrote George Clark, chief protagonist of the grassroots contingent. "This independence makes it possible to reach out to the hearts and minds of ordinary people …" The grassrooters, for their part, while notionally in favour of allowing a hundred flowers to bloom, were particularly hostile to the small (some said "elitist") group which tried to make sense of nuclear strategy and foreign policy and tried to see whether there wasn't a chance for the CND to make some kind of impact at that level.

This gathering, the Disarmament and Strategy Group (Dis and Strat), was the brainchild of Peggy Duff. Seeing that Labour support for CND was ebbing (especially after the death of Hugh Gaitskell, the arrival of Harold Wilson, and the alleged need for the Labour boat not to be rocked by CND in the pre-election period), and that the older generation of CND "big names" had shot their bolt, Peggy sought to engage the energies of a younger generation — people who still for the most part at that stage put CND at the top of their own personal political priorities. She took particular pleasure in the apparent establishment nature of her brains trust — Terence Heelas, a member of the Institute for Strategic Studies; Bill Wedderburn, a law professor at the London School of Economics and John Gittings and myself, researchers at the Royal Institute of International Affairs. We met regularly at the Hampstead flat of Sheila Oakes.

Dis and Strat was meant to be a vehicle for the genius of Stuart Hall, in my view CND's most original strategic thinker as well as its most brilliant platform orator. In practice, Stuart went off soon to work in Birmingham, but he left some petards behind, in particular a policy statement entitled *Steps Towards Peace*, written in the aftermath of the Cuba crisis, and at least two issues of a CND quarterly which he edited called *War and Peace*. The magazine was (in part) designed to open a dialogue "between supporters of unilateral nuclear disarmament and others ... who, while not supporting CND, are seriously concerned about the problems of disarmament and peace."

Many campaigners were not keen on that dialogue, probably on the grounds that it appeared to dilute the basic message: "No to nuclear weapons, no to NATO."

Both Stuart Hall's *Steps Towards Peace*, and the pamphlet *NATO's Final Decade* (written by John Gittings and myself for the Disarmament and Strategy Group and published eventually by the London Region CND), while agreeing with CND policy that Britain should leave NATO, discussed what usefully could be done — in terms of arms control and disengagement in Central Europe — before this desirable event happened. And this for many people was heresy.

The rows that these pamphlets generated were I think caused by the very great schism within the movement between those who believed that CND, even though it had failed to convert the Labour Party, still had a capacity for influence and for making its voice heard in the arena of traditional politics, and those who saw CND as a lever for promoting major social and political change. In retrospect I think both were wrong. Dis and Strat provoked some debate with the Fabian Society but not much else, and the Labour Party, once in government, never mentioned disengagement or the Rapacki Plan — the staple diet of CND's defence intellectuals — ever again. The grassrooters, for their part, got stuck in the grassroots and found that people were much more concerned about motorways, poverty and the blacks next door, than they were about the Bomb – let alone NATO.

Yet I think that CND was right to try to be an intensely political organisation, as it was called into existence, not by some deep-seated urge on the part of the British people for peace, but by the nature of the crisis both between East and West and within the two alliance systems in the late 1950s. For a while the CND made an impact and was listened to. But when that particular form of those two crises subsided in the early 1960s, CND inevitably declined – to be replaced by a new protest movement against a more pressing aspect of the overall crisis: the Vietnam War.

Cuba '62: That Was the Week that Was (almost our last)
Nigel Young

There are almost as many reasons given for the decline of CND in the sixties as there were fragments left over. Everyone has their favourite moments when CND began to decline. Or their pet reasons for why it began to fade. For the media it was (of course) internal splits and the beatniks. For Canon John Collins it was Earl Russell and the direct actionists, anarchists and civil disobedience; for Bertrand Russell it was the other way round, the failure of CND in 1959-60 to meet the nuclear challenge seriously and militantly enough. For Peggy Duff, I suspect it was what she called the "vicarious, remote" nature of the leadership she worked for, and the discovery by 1963 that the Labour Party route had proved a cul-de-sac. For others it was the attentions of the Communist Party, especially when they began to make it a serious target as their main peace front after 1963. A reason much favoured both at the time and since, by political commentators, was the over-concern with nuclear testing as a limited negotiable issue which was undermined as a key issue by the Partial Atmospheric Test Ban Treaty of 1963.

But the favourite of almost everyone (who was not in CND) was Cuba week, the missile crisis of October 1962, when we certainly reached the nuclear brink, but didn't (quite) topple over.

For a week we watched the game of bluff, or chicken – which is what deterrence in crisis turned out to be, played out between two global executives. JFK apparently pondered a slide towards catastrophe as he read about the escalation of August 1914. Krushchev "smelt burning in the air". It confirmed in many of us a sense that the nuclear weapons issue was an issue of the long haul; to protest on the brink was mere ritual; the missiles in Turkey were already in the last stages of alert. Best perhaps to make a run for it. But the bluff worked; the deterrent was "credible": it proved that some luck was on the side of the species (at least on one occasion), but little more.

The argument that it was this that precipitated CND's decline, I always find one of the least persuasive – if anything confirmed how right we were, that we were staring Armageddon in the face, it was that showdown in the Atlantic. One false move, and our prophecy would have been fulfilled, no thanks to deterrence; it may be that those who fled to the west of Ireland or the Hebrides were behaving more rationally than those of us who paraded in Grosvenor Square or outside the Russian Embassy. CND did not immediately decline in any case.

The CND demonstrations which greeted the intended installation of forty "defensive" Russian nuclear missiles in the Caribbean, and the American ultimate threat to launch thousands in retaliation, were, though respectable in size, among the least impressive in the first five years of campaigning. There was a palpable sense of impotence and irrelevance both of our actions and our "little Englandist" posture. And yet the role of public opinion was a critical factor in staying the hand of the decision-makers (or so they tell us); the moral opprobrium of nuclear first-use was greater in 1962 than four years earlier, because of CND, and, in the USA, SANE.

Of course, whilst Cuba week confirmed our sense of urgency it did also make us feel more impotent; it exposed our lack of strategy, our lack of success, our lack of allies and linkages at home and internationally. There was nothing we could do except watch our prophecies approach fulfilment. There were also signs of impending splits and new alignments ("Hands off Cuba"), and new priorities for the Left. Yet, was Castro worth a nuclear crisis? I remember a left speaker arguing both that Russia was "adventurist" for putting the missiles there – and "defeatist" for considering taking them away. Fêted by some, Cuba was no non-aligned, non-nuclear socialist paragon; and the political role of Britain and CND was anyway as onlookers. In the torchlight processions there was a sense of belated urgency among some who had not believed our propaganda, and a sense of paralysis amongst those of us who did.

There are some unfavoured reasons of course why CND faded between 1964-79, and I judge them with the benefit of hindsight, to have been equally important to those listed above, though with none of them would I suggest a reduction to single causes. One is a trite piece of political sociology, but true nonetheless. There is a cyclical quality to all social movements, especially those heavily dependent on the young. There is a limit to the number of years that individuals will devote to a single cause, successful or unsuccessful; it will become institutionalised or they will turn to other things, jobs, families, homes and other issues. There was a renewal of growth in CND in early 1963. But the intensity of involvement of 1958-63 could not continue unless the movement evolved and changed and recruited a second generation: it did not – until the 1980s, that is. We might reckon on a similar cycle this time, three years gone and two or three to go.

The other reasons are more political and were recognised by those most politically involved in CND. The first was the lack of an adequate overall political strategy (getting boxed into the left of the Labour Party, or trapped into rhetoric of "filling the jails" were two such failures). Next, we lacked an alternative foreign policy; third, the thorny issue of an alternative to nuclear defence – conventional, unconventional or civilian based, non-military – was one which CND dodged in the 1960s (despite Gene Sharp's and Adam Roberts's cogent proposals).

Together with this was the problem of lowest common denominator policies; the lack of an adequate social theory. These four missing policy elements reflect the failure of the New Left, both within CND and outside, to impress on the movement an adequate synthesis of concerns and visions of change, a convincing overall analysis and a strategy that could set disarmament in the larger and global context and give CND a manifesto. As a result, CND remained –as it was in October 1962, a reactive and single-issue coalition – temporary, diffuse and co-optable.

By 1962 these problems had been recognised by Peggy Duff and those concerned with policy issues: positive neutralism was one response to them – linking up laterally with those outside the great military power blocs. But as Cuba suggested, this was often superficial, if not naïve.

At the very time when unilateralism needed to internationalise itself – and this crisis was symptomatic of the need for a non-aligned transnational response – we still held narrowly nationalist, aligned or isolationist stances. Admittedly one response was to look again at incremental and reciprocal initiatives including nuclear free zones; but *Steps Towards Peace*, produced after Cuba week, which stressed graduated disarmament especially in Europe, was interpreted (rightly in my view) as throwing out the unilateralist core of a new foreign and defence policy. Moreover, it was a policy for governments, not popular movements; it underplayed the role of non-governmental organisations and communities (something perhaps we have learnt after twenty years?).

More genuinely promising was the nonaligned internationalism of the International Confederation of Disarmament and Peace (ICDP), which Peggy helped found in 1962-3. It came too little and too late, and was (in my view) subsequently compromised by the war in Indo-China. A genuine transnational anti-nuclear mood, at least in Europe, has had to wait until the 1980s – when the possibility of movements crossing the great military ideological divides, East and West, at least has a chance of success. The dangers of another Cuba week have not disappeared in the past twenty years. What we can learn from it in the 1980s is the necessity for a globalist vision of change, a strategy for the longer term, in which the peace movement moves from a negative reactive motivation, towards the empowerment of constituencies which can pre-empt such crises, and re-possess power over political conditions which make such events possible. The women's encirclement of Greenham is a symbol of that potential.

Greece '63
John Petherbridge

A prominent Greek politician is murdered in Salonika. The Greek Prime Minister resigns over his Royal Family's desire to visit Britain. During that visit the Queen of England is booed in the streets of London. And some months later an over-zealous police officer is proved to have planted half bricks on innocent demonstrators. The year was 1963, and all these events followed the banning of the first Marathon to Athens Peace March and the deportation of some of the British contingent who had gone to Greece to participate. I was one of the deportees.

The March was organised by the Bertrand Russell Committee of 100. The Committee had been set up by Michael Peristerakis, a law student at Athens University, after he had published a peace manifesto during the 1962 Cuban missile crisis. There was already a Greek Peace Committee, but its membership was almost exclusively from the left-wing EDA party and its policies were seen as being heavily biased towards the Soviet Union. Peristerakis was not a member of EDA and was determined that the new movement should be unaligned. But sometimes this fear of being too closely associated with the left led to political vagueness. The Bertrand Russell Committee was against nuclear bases on Greek soil and the use of Greek ports by American Polaris submarines, but had an ambiguous attitude to NATO and to unilateralism. The popularity of the Bertrand Russell Committee was due to an emotional desire for peace rather than to its policies – not surprising in a country still recovering from a disastrous civil war between left and right.

John Chambers, a Committee of 100 activist, organised a small British contingent to participate in the Marathon to Athens Easter Peace March. I answered his small-ad in *Peace News* which suggested the trip would be as much a holiday as a demonstration of international solidarity. At the time I worked as an articled clerk for a firm of accountants. There my CND activities were regarded either with hostility or as a bizarre eccentricity. Greece couldn't have been more different: Peristerakis and the other male leaders, always to be seen in suits, shirts and ties, would not have been out of place at my office.

Twelve days before the march we arrived in Athens at six in the morning. There were more than forty members of the Bertrand Russell Committee waiting to welcome us. Earlier there had been hundreds but our train was four hours late. Immediately we were taken to a pre-breakfast press conference. It was a foretaste of the attention that was to be lavished on us during our visit. Everywhere we were treated with great warmth and friendliness. The meetings we attended were packed. Just the mention of having been on Aldermaston Marches brought spontaneous applause, and Bertrand Russell seemed to be nearly everybody's favourite Englishman.

Three days before the march, I was arrested and taken to police headquarters. I was photographed, fingerprinted and then released four hours later. Two days later I was arrested again. At police headquarters I was forcibly searched and questioned about the demonstration, which the government had banned although there was an article in the Greek Constitution stating the right to demonstrate. I refused to answer any questions. One of the plain-clothes men said, "We have ways of making you talk." I laughed.

A man said to be in charge entered the room. The blinds on the window were lowered. A subordinate removed my spectacles. The new arrival slapped me hard across the face and then departed without saying anything. My glasses were returned and I was put in a bare cell. To pass the time I scratched a large CND symbol on the wall with a coin.

Two hours later I was taken upstairs to join the other arrested members of our group. We were kept together in a large room with hard benches, an open door and an armed guard. Late in the afternoon John Chambers and his wife were taken to the airport and eventually deported. During the night more British supporters arrived, having been arrested when their train reached Athens.

The next morning, Sunday, the day of the march, I alone was taken by jeep to what I was told was the alien's prison. No one explained why I had been singled out. I stayed there all day. None of the other prisoners spoke English but I managed to tell them who I was by drawing another large symbol on a prison wall. Finally, that evening, I was taken to the station and put on a train. Armed guards kept me company till we reached the Yugoslav frontier.

That Sunday more than 800 other people were arrested for trying to take part in the march. One man, Gregory Lambrakis, completed the full distance. His membership of the Greek Parliament gave him immunity from arrest. A month later he was deliberately knocked down by a motorcycle combination after addressing a peace meeting in Salonika. He died from his injuries. His funeral brought a quarter of a million people on to the streets in what was the first major political demonstration for several years.

The visit of Queen Fredericka and King Paul to Britain in July of that year was seen by many in CND as an attempt to buy political respectability for the Greek regime. Demonstrations seemed likely, and Prime Minister Karamanlis recommended that the visit should be postponed. His advice was ignored so he resigned.

Two days before the visit, CND held a march in memory of Lambrakis. During the visit, the Committee of 100 organised demonstrations under the heading "Against Tyranny". At one of these the Queen was booed, to the apoplectic horror of the *Daily Mail*, and false evidence was planted on non-violent demonstrators.

Some CND supporters felt that such demonstrations were irrelevant, that they courted unnecessary unpopularity and fatally broadened the aims of the Campaign. A letter-writer in *Peace News* described them as part of a "feud being waged against the Greek Royal Family". But such demonstrations were one of the few ways of putting pressure on the Greek government who had banned some peace activities such as the Marathon to Athens March. It was the Greek Peace Movement that had asked us to show our support. Greece was also a member of NATO and the Royal visit was an opportunity to expose the hypocrisy of a nuclear alliance which claimed to defend freedom and democracy but did nothing to end oppression within one of its member nations — a fact further underlined four years later when the Colonels seized power and NATO did nothing to stop them. And for many of us, who had been in Greece, the demonstrations were a gesture of international solidarity and thanks for the hospitality we'd received during our stay.

Stamina – a main requirement
Dick Nettleton

Over the last two decades writing the history of CND has become a popular pastime. Learned professors and schoolchildren alike have all joined in the fun. In extreme cases the potted histories took the form of obituaries. Like that of Mark Twain they all tended to be premature. As the North West Organiser of CND in the mid-Sixties I often had to divert attention from urgent campaigns to deny media reports of our demise. For instance, on the eve of the 1964 Easter March just as we were finalising the arrangements for several coaches and other transport down to London, a local TV station put out a programme with the opening line "CND is dead at last"; then followed a script full of necrophilic references. I tried for some time to persuade the writer of that script to meet me, but he never responded. Possibly he was afraid of ghosts! I often see his name on the captions when watching the weekend football reviews.

CND has hardly been going long enough to have a history, but it does seem to have a soft spot for a kind of instant nostalgia. When I started to move around Campaign groups in 1963 as the newly appointed organiser of the North West CND, I was somewhat startled to hear references to "the good old days". They meant 1958 and the first Aldermaston March! However, providing it is not taken too seriously, reminiscence can be fun and, to a limited degree, helpful.

By and large, it is more beneficial for the young to learn *in practice* from their own mistakes as each generation resents any attempt by its elders to rob them of this privilege. In our new, lively local peace group, I can see the eyes glaze over when I launch into some tale of the Sixties.

I proceed with great care, therefore, to mention two or three points, albeit that they may seem obvious or even simplistic.

Any movement which has to survive through several generations will not reach its goal by simple arithmetical progression; and yet I constantly meet those who are downcast if the next meeting is not bigger than the last, this year's conference has less delegates than last year's and there are less marchers in the Autumn than in the Spring. When this happens, of course, it is necessary to examine why and learn from the experience, but it should never be a signal for panic and the advocacy of liquidation. It follows that one of the main requirements for a movement whose prime aim is to secure the survival of the human race is that very stamina which we know the race possesses.

There have been and will be in the future many temptations to divert on to matters not directly related to the abolition of weapons of mass destruction; or to issues which are related, but might at the time also have a more immediate appeal.

In the Sixties Vietnam was such an issue. There were those in CND who thought that Vietnam "was nothing to do with us" and did not concede that it might escalate into nuclear war. Conversely there were some supporters who thought that we should put our campaign against Polaris (which was being made in Britain at the time) on ice and concentrate all our efforts on Vietnam. As always, there were all shades of opinion between these positions. Ten or more years later it can hardly be expected that everyone would now agree that all our actions and pronouncements on Vietnam were 100 per cent correct, but I think it can be claimed that CND at least played its part in eventually bringing peace there, and an end to decades of foreign rule.

However, no matter what "other" issues arise, it will always be the job of CND to remind people of the overriding need to get rid of weapons of mass destruction as an essential prerequisite to an enduring peace and a better life.

In the Sixties we were often faced with contradictory tendencies within the movement. The Test Ban Treaty and the avoidance of nuclear war over Cuba were partial victories, but for some this was enough to lull them into complacency or send them off looking for other issues. On the other hand there were some who thought that the reversal of the 1960 Labour Party Conference decision on unilateral nuclear disarmament, and the failure of the 1964 Labour Government to honour its election pledge not to build Polaris, meant that "CND had failed". There were even a few individuals who managed to embrace contradictory outlooks at the same time! But CND managed to survive the contradictions, and I must confess to a great deal of sheer hedonist pleasure when the Campaign revived in the Eighties. We *shall* overcome.

CHAPTER THREE
New Roots in the 1970s

In retrospect, a good deal of the groundwork for CND's huge growth in the 1980s can be traced back to the 1970s. New campaigning ideas, renewed stamina and new issues linked up with our basic opposition to nuclear weapons. **Zoë Fairbairns** recalls how she investigated military research in British universities. **Ian Davison** explains how the Campaign revived in Scotland from the early 1970s. **Duncan Rees** looks particularly at the making of CND's Open Door TV programme and at the intensified use of *The War Game*. **Cathy Ashton** shows how proposals for the neutron bomb helped to rekindle the whole campaign against nuclear war plans. **Val Stevens** traces ways in which the environmental movement of the 1970s came to add a fresh wave of opposition to nuclear weapons.

Study War No More
Zoë Fairbairns

1973-4, when I was editor of *Sanity*, was a fairly lean time for CND. When strangers asked me who I worked for, I always felt I had to spell it out: "CND, that's the Campaign for Nuclear Disarmament, yes, it is still going." There were times when the only people on pickets seemed to be the (four) office staff – does this make us paid agitators, we wondered, as we trooped disconsolately up and down outside the French embassy.

For the editorial board of *Sanity*, major concerns were reduced sales, increased production costs, and a lack of new stories. Articles about Hiroshima Day, or the coming decision on Trident, or conflict in the Labour Party over the bomb, or the Ministry of Defence telling fibs, were all important and interesting; but they had been done before.

Someone suggested an investigative piece on military sponsorship of scientific research in British universities and colleges. It was an issue that had radicalised many students in the USA. In Britain there *were* active student CND groups, but not many; "the bomb" was old hat. It seems incredible now, in 1982, that we had to work so hard, so recently, to make CND appear "relevant" to students already politically active on such matters as apartheid, Northern Ireland, feminism; but it was necessary, and identifying links between the military and academic establishments was how we hoped to do it.

How could we find out about military sponsorship? This was the Watergate era, with government-toppling revelations being whispered to investigative journalists in car parks ... it therefore took a while for it to occur to me to ring up the Ministry of Defence and ask them.

They obligingly provided me with a list that showed that nearly every university in the country was doing its bit towards the production of military hardware. University annual reports soon revealed that sponsored projects ranged from work on helicopters, lasers, computers, explosives and metals under stress, to work on malaria, motion-sickness, skin-irritants, drugs metabolism and people under stress. There were also Ministry of Defence-funded lectureships at five universities, and a network of "Military Education Committees", co-ordinated by the MoD and concerned to promote better relations between the academic and military communities; and there were projects sponsored by NATO and by the United States Department of Defence.

The MoD assured me that "only a small proportion" of their sponsored research was secret. A few months later, they denied, to the *Daily Telegraph*, that they did any secret work at all in universities; but I certainly encountered a number of university scientists who felt they were "not allowed" to discuss what they were doing for the Ministry. Others stoutly denied that their military-funded work had any military implications: "This will be used to prevent explosions in coal mines," a straight-faced departmental secretary told me at Cambridge, referring to a project on the initiation of explosions which was being jointly funded by the MoD and the US Army.

Others felt it their patriotic duty to do military research, others again felt that it didn't matter who funded them because their work was so basic that it could be put to dozens of uses, military or otherwise.

But some scientists were not so complacent. One, at Manchester, told me of his distress, after accepting a grant from the US Department of Defence for a project concerned with cloud-seeding, to read that artificial rain had been used as a weapon of war in Vietnam. A research fellow at Liverpool University resigned his post in the Department of Electrical Engineering and Electronics when his supervisor suggested that he co-operate with military research establishments. A Belfast professor expressed surprise when his US-Navy-funded project on "interstellar matter" appeared in an official US list of research projects under the heading, "Nuclear Weaponry." Another scientist wrote to me:

"Not all military grants are for military purposes ... nevertheless, I realise that the aim of some of these grants, however harmless they may seem, could be to enlist the help of scientists if more urgent military matters were to turn up."

When CND revealed these findings – in two special student issues of *Sanity*, and the pamphlet *Study War No More* – there was a lot of interest, both in the national press and among students. Many students' unions contacted us for more information; we then urged them to conduct their own investigations at a local level. The research groups they set up were often either based on CND groups, or developed into CND groups, or took on an anti-militarist commitment which was not necessarily the same as CND's, but had a lot in common with it.

Not all who were led to reconsider their position on militarism by the discovery that someone was developing weapons in their own college lab, joined CND; not everyone in CND found a campaign against military research strictly relevant. Pacifists opposed any kind of war-preparation, but those who restricted their aims to *nuclear* disarmament had no special reason for objecting to the development of conventional arms, in universities or anywhere else. People who saw militarism primarily as a class issue did not see much reason to differentiate between military sponsorship of research, and sponsorship by civilian businesses who make anti-social products.

I think we did not really resolve these questions, and that's why, although a number of groups (e.g. at Leeds, Liverpool, Manchester and Southampton) produced exhaustive reports and organised actions around their own institutions' military connections, a major national campaign did not develop.

But the way is open for such a campaign. Anyone wanting to know about military research in a particular university should first consult the annual report; find the names of the people concerned; and for further information, *ask them*. At the very least, such investigations bring up important questions of responsibility, secrecy, morality; and they make real what we all have to know – that weapons don't invent themselves.

The Scottish Revival
Ian Davison

At the beginning of the 1970s, CND in Scotland was just as weak as in the rest of the UK. One or two members went down to the annual conference, and we had a representative on National Council. Occasionally, someone would breathe life into a local CND group, sell pamphlets, or feed lonely resolutions into political parties, councils or trades unions. *Sanity* carried articles from Scotland; a few people went round delivering it; many of us did no more than read it – if that!

But underneath the general apathy, wide support for nuclear disarmament lived on. The memories of the anti-Polaris campaign were vivid and the songs were still sung.

Some people now pinned their anti-nuclear hopes on the revived Scottish National Party. But in almost all the political parties, trade unions, churches and community organisations, there were key people, in their thirties and forties, who were increasingly influential and who had first seen political daylight at Aldermaston. The large (but usually emigrant) Scottish wayes in the "drop-out" flood also retained a lot of affection for CND (and the Committee of 100). Some of these currents flowed together briefly, on the initiative of Morris Blythman, for a Glasgow-to-Holy-Loch motorcade and rally in 1971.

But the tide turned in 1972/3. British CND decided to hold its next main demo (traditionally at Easter) away from the South East, especially Aldermaston. There was a hunch that in 1973 Scotland could provide the first growth-point in this public side of our campaigning. CND decided to show up the full Clydeside complex of nuclear weapons bases, by going to the British Polaris base at Faslane, rather than to the already notorious US base at Holy Loch.

The Scottish ground was sown very carefully in the autumn of 1972, by John Cox and Dick Nettleton from the South, to make sure of all-party support (except Tory). This headed off the bitter sectarianism which sometimes disgraces Scottish radical politics. The demonstration was a fair size for a two-day event: the cheerful atmosphere, the music and the hospitality in Clydebank made a strong impact. There was a "peace-train" from London and an "exorcism" at the Faslane base by Bruce Kent. Ian Munro's overall organisation was brilliant, with excellent help from trade unions and local authorities.

A whole series of Clydeside demos for nuclear disarmament followed over the next eight years, and most benefitted from the lessons of that 1973 success: they were imaginative, they were carefully planned and budgetted, and they involved early inter-party political preparation. The next time everything clicked quite as well was when we organised a Peace Cruise to Holy Loch in September 1977 (after 1973, we steered clear of Easter for our main event. This avoided close comparisons with the Aldermaston legend; and it enabled the handful of really keen people to support both an English Easter event and a Scottish summer demo!).

But in between these public spasms, a steady base of local activity was built up. In the summer of 1973, Scottish CND was re-formed. A solid foundation of affiliations, especially from trade unions, was laid down; and a unique "regional" membership scheme was started. CND activities were fostered first in the main cities and the colleges. For stability, with limited resources, the Scottish CND Committee had a clear Glasgow base, with a small office, regular fund-raising jumble sales and weekly street-petitioning from April to September. We sent out a two-monthly newsletter and held a general meeting of Scottish CND at least every six months and not always in Glasgow.

We were well aware of weaknesses. There was a crying need for simple literature, but we produced little Scottish material. Our press work was very weak after 1973. Our organised contact with youth and with women, especially housewives, was poor, and our work in the churches was hesitant for several reasons: much church opinion was hostile to our message, while those who were sympathetic within had their own separate peace groups.

When our message was accepted, our image was still rather "left-wing".

Films were quickly found to be a success: we followed Yorkshire CND's example and bought our own copy of *The War Game*. Other fruitful activities were our interventions of various kinds, at trade union and nationalist events, and at ecology occasions which were making the word "nuclear" better understood.

A vital ingredient for Scottish CND's steady growth in the 1970s was diversity: diversity of individual members who worked together, and diversity of activities. And of these activities, one of the most valuable was one of the least spectacular — street-petitioning.

Street-petitioning was done mostly on Saturday afternoons, especially in the centres of Glasgow and Aberdeen. It gave us a wide audience of ordinary people who would never have come looking for us. It gave us a regular weekly income from countless and painless 10p donations. It gave us an outlet for huge numbers of badges, leaflets and other literature. It let us persuade the most interested people to join us in activity. And it told us quickly how public opinion was responding to events and media reports over the years — French open-air nuclear tests, the neutron bomb, early talk of Cruise missiles, the NATO "modernisation" decisions and so on.

If you want to be in touch with the (wo)man-in-the-street, you've got to be there!

The Tide Turns
Duncan Rees

"CND GROWS!" proclaimed the banner headline of *Sanity* in February 1977; and although the basis for this view may have been tenuous compared to the advances we can claim for the 1980s, there was certainly by then a feeling in the Campaign that the tide was beginning to turn in CND's favour. As CND Chairman, John Cox, said at the 1976 annual conference, the Campaign had got over "that dreadful period of being a huge organisation declining. We are now a small organisation that is growing".

One factor which had helped CND in 1976 had been the opportunity to make our TV programme *All Against the Bomb* for BBC-2 as part of their "Open Door" community access series. The results of making the film were both beneficial, and at the same time a salutary warning that we should be under no illusions about the alleged "impartiality" of certain sections of the media. The film was several months in the making and was first shown on 1 October 1976 (we had first applied for an Open Door slot in 1973!). I suspect that most involved in making the film would now look back and recognise its deficiencies — especially compared to some of the excellent material produced since that time. Nevertheless, the screening of *All Against the Bomb* revealed what we had always believed, namely that there *was* a large untapped potential support for CND in the country. We received several thousand enquiries in response to the programme, and estimated that around two hundred new members were gained as a direct result. This was despite the late scheduling of the programme – 11.15 pm on BBC-2 not being exactly peak viewing time! – and also despite the partially successful attempts by BBC and Ministry of Defence to censor the film.

We had always intended to make the point in the film that lack of attention in the media had resulted in an unbalanced coverage of disarmament issues, with the proponents of the status quo getting most benefit from what coverage there was. But after we had completed the film, just a few weeks before it was due to be screened, the BBC made our point for us by insisting that we make cuts in certain sequences. We had intended to include extracts from a BBC current affairs programme in which Polaris crew members talked about how *they* saw the responsibility of having at their fingertips the power to destroy millions of people. One of the men says "come the day, we wouldn't ever hesitate, we'd run into a prearranged drill and it would, hopefully, work like clockwork" ... And later: "The idea of firing at civilians doesn't really cross my mind, er, because I believe the deterrent works" – this from one of the Polaris captains. This material (and more) was deemed too sensitive by the authorities; as the *Daily Express* reported – the MoD was "incensed", and the BBC, accepting that there had been pressure from the MoD, insisted, despite our protests, on making the cuts.

The BBC's censorship of CND's Open Door programme contained a supreme irony; in that same year CND had bought a copy of *The War Game* – the famous BBC film about a nuclear attack on Britain, written and directed by Peter Watkins in 1965, but of course banned from TV screens by yet another example of media suppression. We had in fact even been refused permission to use excerpts from *The War Game* in our Open Door programme. And it had always seemed certain to us, that government, MoD or Home Office pressure had played a major part in the BBC's decision to suppress the film.

So we set out, in 1976 and '77, to try to see if *The War Game* could live up to the expectations bestowed upon it many years earlier: *The Observer* had said: "It may be the most important film ever made. We are always being told that works of art cannot change the course of history. I believe this one might ... it should be screened everywhere on earth." The effect of *The War Game*, in 1977 no less than in 1965, was to expose the horror and futility of thermo-nuclear war, and, as Peter Watkins puts it "help break the present silence existing in most forms of communication on the entire, complex subject of thermo-nuclear weapons – their policies and their effects." Our (CND's) experience at countless meetings with the film was that it shocks, can even cause despair, but that most importantly it helps to arouse concern about the urgent need to work for the abolition of nuclear weapons.

The BBC, however, in a seemingly contemptuous attitude towards their viewers, claimed in 1977 that The War Game "could produce a wholly irrational reaction among many members of the audience ... " No doubt the government would also view the likely response to the film as being "irrational". But for "irrational" read "socially and politically motivated". Then, in those four words, I think we see the real reason for the supression of the film – a fearful establishment, uncertain even of its own arguments.

Our countrywide weeks of action involving showings of The War Game certainly provided a stimulus for the Campaign during the late 1970s. The film, combined with speakers and other activities, attracted many new members, led to the formation of a number of new CND groups, and helped to generate enthusiasm and activity – which had been less in evidence before this when CND had largely restricted itself to the more modest aspirations of a small pressure group.

That pressure-group style of work was never abandoned, and in fact became even more important as the campaign grew; but the figures produced for CND's 1978 annual conference in Manchester spoke for themselves, as far as getting the message out to the public in a campaigning style was concerned: there had been over 160 major showings of The War Game during the year – some attended by very large audiences (e.g. 800 at Liverpool University); CND had records of 102 local groups around the country, compared to 60 two years previously; and in the two years up to November 1978 that CND had been using The War Game, it was estimated that around 20,000 people had seen the film and heard the accompanying CND speakers. This of course was happening in a climate of political and current affairs that was still not really helpful to CND, although the neutron bomb issue was soon to start changing all that. In the meantime, we continued to make progress; from 1972, in which year CND recruited only 105 new national members in the whole country, we moved up to 440 new members in 1976 and 569 and 602 in 1977 and 1978 respectively. Many of these new members were young people – which not only made for a vital addition to the 'sturdy veterans' of the campaign, but which also perhaps reflected the fact that by this time CND's full time staff were all themselves relatively youthful, and starting careers – not a bad thing for a campaign which still needed to shake off much of its early-Sixties' image and move forward with new ideas and activities.

There is a great deal which could be said about CND in the late 1970s, and perhaps many lessons to be learned – especially since this was the phase of changing approach and modest expansion which immediately preceded CND's big take off in the early 1980s.

But, crucial to this period was that while moving in new directions, with new strategies and ways of campaigning and an infusion of new people, we never tossed aside the better methods and principles which had stood us in good stead through lean years before; nor was "age and experience" ditched in favour of exuberance and youth, or vice versa! If this should be one of the hallmarks of a broad-based non-sectarian campaign – then CND will never fail to gain by learning from, but not being dominated by, its history.

The End of the '70s – the beginning of the revival
Cathy Ashton

By the mid-1970s, the Campaign was at a stage where it desperately needed a new impetus. People had learned to accept the bomb, if indeed they thought about it at all. Audiences could still be found to listen to the message, but it seemed that there was a futility and remoteness about the issue which could not be broken. An apparent lack of innovation in the arms race made a sense of complacency, if not security, even more prevalent.

Sadly, much of the impetus so badly needed to revive CND came from the 1977 decision to introduce a weapon to the nuclear arsenals that dramatically demonstrated the change in NATO's policy on the deployment of nuclear weapons. There is little doubt that the prospect of the neutron bomb awoke the population of Britain once again to the dangers of nuclear war. The main claim to fame of the neutron bomb came from the sometimes exaggerated fact of its proportionately higher emission of radiation as compared with the effects of blast, heat and fallout – the four constituent "parts" of a nuclear bomb. This weapon would therefore be potentially more lethal to living things within a given area than to buildings. Linked to this decision to introduce a new kind of nuclear weapon was the daunting proposition that this tactical nuclear weapon would be controlled by commanders in the battlefield. The concept of "pressing the buttons in Washington and Moscow when all else had failed" had gone, and instead there was a realisation that nuclear strategy had come to think the unthinkable – that to fight a nuclear war was an active possibility.

Throughout Europe, President Carter's decision to deploy this weapon unwittingly created the seed from which the European peace movement was to blossom. In 1978, following some way behind the example of the Dutch, CND in Britain launched its neutron bomb petition. A quarter of a million signatures were collected in the next few months. While not matching Holland's million signatures, this helped to create the political climate which led Carter to announce that the deployment of the bomb would be deferred. Significantly for CND, it became clear that united action within Europe was capable of achieving results.

However, the neutron bomb decision did not mean any more than it said.

The potential for the bomb to be deployed later was still there. But for CND, the neutron bomb had aroused public interest and – an important aid to campaigning – media attention. The opportunity arose to explain where the neutron bomb fitted into an overall strategy – a strategy which few realised had changed. President Nixon had ratified the policy of Counterforce, moving on from the 1960s' strategy of Mutually Assured Destruction (MAD) where neither side would willingly fight because of the other's ability to destroy it. Instead, the concept of a flexible response to aggression had moved the world a little closer to the possibility of war: it hardly need be said that one of the responses might well be nuclear. Coupled to this was the notion of fighting a "limited" nuclear war – with the whole of Europe being the battlefield! Campaigning continued – but with new momentum.

The growth of European links was an important aspect of the campaigning which followed over the next few years. For a long time the only connections had been via an international conference circuit where a few people had represented CND, among other organisations. The work that these people had done to make sure that CND was kept firmly "on the map" internationally should not be understated; but it was now possible for CND to link directly with grassroots movements in Europe, starting particularly in Holland.

Invitations came for CND to participate in activities such as the Dutch-initiated visit to the United Nations in 1979. Representatives from movements in Finland, East and West Germany, Poland and Canada (among others) met to present a declaration on disarmament. While in the USA, they took part in demonstrations and meetings, and met with peace groups working particularly in Washington and New York. Our participation in these events confirmed that we were not alone, and that the groundswell of anti-nuclear campaigning was already powerful in Europe, as it was becoming in Britain. From these small beginnings were to grow international demonstrations such as that in Brussels at Easter 1981.

While concern was growing over the whole NATO strategy on nuclear weapons, CND's campaigning also continued on the question of Britain's independent nuclear "deterrent". As early as the mid-1970s CND was opposing proposals for the Polaris replacement. The issue had always been a focal point for campaigning in Scotland, where the Polaris submarines are based; but it was not until Trident, massively dangerous and expensive, was an integral part of the new government's policies that it became a campaigning focus throughout Britain.

As Trident became part of the government's defence policy for Britain, so the deployment of Cruise missiles became a part of the defence policy of NATO. In December 1979, NATO ministers decided to site Cruise missiles throughout Europe in 1983. A whole range of local campaigns sprang up across Britain against the missiles, and by the end of 1980 many of these campaigns had become part of CND.

In many ways CND is not the movement it was in the late 1970s – certainly its growth has been terrific. However, the Campaign in the '70s should not be dismissed. There was, in fact, massive support – though much of it was dormant. Many felt there was little point in campaigning on the issue as it seemed impossible to achieve anything: there was not enough sense of urgency. Perhaps the biggest change in thinking has been the realisation that the abolition of nuclear weapons is essential to the survival of mankind and that this overshadows any other issue in the 1980s. But those who worked through the 1970s did maintain the foundations on which the new movement could be built.

The importance of the environmental movement
Val Stevens

The growth of the Ecology movement in the early seventies, with the setting up of the Conservation Society, Friends of the Earth (FOE), Greenpeace, then the Ecology Party, and, later, the Socialist Environment and Resources Association, took place when the early massive CND movement had dwindled.

Perhaps people felt that world extermination by nuclear weapons had been excluded by universal fear of using them: anyway, it seemed that there were more ways than one of destroying life on earth. Population growth and the impact that was having on water supplies, fuel and energy supplies, agricultural practices, and on finite resources in general; plus the spin-off in terms of mounting pollution of air, land and sea; all these loomed as insidious, but certain means of destroying our life-support systems. For environmentalists, "the bomb" became *one* of the routes to destruction of the planet, but by no means an overriding one – more a nagging anxiety pushed to the back of one's mind.

However, even then, environmentalists in the UK were taking note of the findings of Linus Pauling on additional cancer and leukaemia deaths resulting from atmospheric nuclear bomb *testing*. After the 1963 Test Ban Treaty agreement to conduct nuclear tests underground, it was mainly the French who continued to carry out surface testing, in the South Pacific, incurring widespread anger. In 1971, the *Ecologist* (UK environmental journal) carried an extensive article on the social and environmental damage being caused by fall-out from the tests. In 1973 the New Zealand Prime Minister decided to sail into the French test area as a protest.

By the mid-Seventies, Australia had become a world leader in the fight against nuclear technology, with environmentalists and trade unions combining for the first time, to arrive at a position where a ban was placed on the mining, handling and shipment of uranium. This was partly because people were aware of the plight of the aborigines, whose lands would be destroyed, and partly because they knew that shipments of uranium could contribute to the nuclear weapons build-up.

Such developments filtered back to the UK, and the Environmental movement began to understand anew the danger of radiation to living cells. So it began seriously to question the safety of nuclear power plants and associated processes. The first major critique – by Walt Patterson, FOE Consultant on energy matters – appeared in the *Ecologist* in 1973. (However, it did not mention any connection with nuclear weapons).

In spite of this, the UK environmentalists were too busy with the issues of self-sufficiency, organic agriculture, returnable bottles and saving whales (and Wales, from RTZ!) to take the issue very seriously. Not until 1975, when the Australian uranium ban hit the headlines, and Amory Lovins (FOE, USA) published a definitive work, *Non-Nuclear Futures*, did the issue become a campaigning one. Lovins did make the link – "We hide from ourselves that it is the same atom, whether in fist or glove". Eeven then, at an FOE energy workshop in 1976, largely concerned with nuclear energy, no decision could be taken as to whether FOE should support the CND position on nuclear weapons. Patterson argued that much more discussion and information was needed.

Yet under the mountain of publications about nuclear energy, the weapons issue was alive and kicking. The *Flowers Report* (Royal Commission on Environmental Pollution – Nuclear Power), 1976, laid great stress on the possible diversion of nuclear material for weapons use. The theme of "The Plutonium Economy" was expanded by Peter Bunyard in the *Ecologist*, as the Windscale planning application for a massive new reprocessing plant came into the news.

At the subsequent Windscale inquiry (1977) according to the official inquiry report, "The spread of nuclear weapons capability was much canvassed ... It formed the main ground upon which FOE submitted that a decision on the building of the plant should be delayed for 10 years."

Since the Windscale inquiry it has been increasingly difficult for environmental organisations to ignore the nuclear weapons issue. FOE has supported all major CND events, and CND has supported FOE's demonstrations on nuclear energy. However, the Conservation Society has had more problems: during the past year its executive came out in support of CND, only to be opposed by a referendum of its members. As a compromise it has affiliated to the World Disarmament Campaign, whose demands are less specific.

Meanwhile, all over Britain, groups have taken up nuclear energy, either as a general issue or as a local one – opposition to the Torness Reactor or the Heysham one; opposition to nuclear waste being transported through cities;

protest against dumping nuclear waste at sea or underground; and, among more political groups, opposition to nuclear technology contracts with such countries as Brazil, and South Africa, and to the import of uranium from Namibia, with its overtones of South African oppression.

Throughout Europe the anti-nuclear power movement, with its universal symbol of the smiling sun, has developed a style of campaigning, of camps and occupations, of citizens' actions, of withholding electricity bills, which has caught people's imagination. In Britain the events have generally been less spectacular, but even where demonstrators only number a dozen or so, the techniques of street theatre, radiation suits, die-ins, and so on, win much attention from the media. A group in Bristol even went to the lengths of stopping a train shipping low-level waste to the docks.

One result of all this disparate anti-nuclear activity was the formation of the Anti-Nuclear Campaign at the end of 1979. It was to act as an umbrella for much of the grassroots protest. It was more of a radical, trade-union orientated body than its predecessors, and less concerned with general environmental matters. It concentrated on safety issues, radiation hazards, civil and trade-union liberties and rights; by 1980 it had adopted the aim of stopping nuclear weapons as an equal priority to stopping nuclear power. An important element in CND's massive resurgence has been this increasing wish to extend the anti-nuclear power movement to oppose nuclear weapons.

CHAPTER FOUR
The Upsurge since 1980

CND's resurgence in the 1980s had distinct but overlapping aspects. **Edward Thompson** places this resurgence in its European context, and outlines the work of END. **Alison Whyte** offers a view of the part being played by women in the struggle for nuclear disarmament. **Philip Bolsover** describes new developments in civil defence. **Sheila Oakes** reviews the range and role of other organisations that comprise, with CND, the wider peace movement; and **Joan Ruddock** gives reasons for the Campaign's revival and suggests priorities for the future.

Resurgence in Europe, and the rôle of END
Edward Thompson

After the great demonstrations in European cities in October and November 1981 – in which some two millions took part – President Reagan announced that "those are all sponsored by a thing called the World Peace Council, which is bought and paid for by the Soviet Union". Vladimir Bukovsky, a Soviet dissident and émigré who was appallingly treated by the Soviet security authorities and who is, understandably, deeply embittered by the experience, has offered to provide chapter and verse for this theory. In an article in *Commentary* (May 1982) he disclosed that it was all planned at a conference of the World Peace Council in Sofia in September 1980.

I was not at that Sofia conference, and in two and a half years of campaigning, which has taken me to many parts of Europe and introduced me to hundreds of European activists, I cannot recall talking to anyone who was. My own account of the sequence of events will be very different.

What "orchestrated" the new European movement was the NATO modernisation decision of 12 December 1979: since this involved five recipient nations as harbours for cruise missiles or Pershing IIs (Britain, Holland, Belgium, West Germany and Italy), and involved other NATO partners (notably the Scandinavian countries) as accessories to the fact. This multi-national NATO strategy inevitably summoned into existence a multi-national campaign of resistance.

I was recruited to the new movement in the autumn of 1979 not by the Russians but by some BBC television defence "expert". I was in the middle of writing a series of dismal articles for *New Society* on "The State of the Nation" when I switched on the box and was informed, in the blandest possible way, that NATO had prepared this wonderful new package for us and that "we" were anxious to take our full share of these fearsomely-dangerous weapons – and more than our share if the Dutch should prove to have "moral objections" to taking theirs. This gave me the conclusion to my articles; and the commencement of a new life of campaigning.

Although I had taken my share in the early years of CND I had, like many others of that generation, lapsed my activity (and membership). I was dimly aware that something called SALT treaties were being negotiated, and supposed (mistakenly) that these had something to do with making nuclear weapons either safer or less. The BBC's "expert" cleared my mind, and I applied it to catching up on some neglected reading – like Alva Myrdal's *The Game of Disarmament*.

The British were slow to understand what was happening in the autumn of 1979: even Parliament was not consulted before the NATO decision. And we were slow to mount a campaign of opposition. The Dutch and the Norwegians were the first to do this. By December the telephone and post were humming, and various strategies were being canvassed for getting some new-style movement going. Then came the Soviet invasion of Afghanistan and the prospect seemed hopeless. Some people with whom we had been having discussions pulled back sharply and said that the moment for a peace campaign was inopportune.

Opportune or not, the rising tension brought about by Afghanistan and the NATO decision made peace campaigning necessary and urgent. END, or European Nuclear Disarmament, really came into being in February 1980. A group of us were in regular correspondence and a consensus emerged. We did not go, first of all, to CND because it seemed that single nationally-based movements were no longer adequate. There must be an international response, with some common programme, to meet an international threat. This programme must be clearly non-aligned: it must favour neither bloc. The SS-20s as well as cruise missiles must be opposed. I think that it was Ken Coates, of the Bertrand Russell Peace Foundation, who first proposed on the phone that the essence of the programme must be a call for all nuclear weapons to be cleared out of Europe, East and West: all manufacture: all sites: and all weapons targeted upon Europe. I wrote the first draft of the END Appeal, and it was then knocked about and greatly revised, to its advantage, by my wife, Dorothy; by Ken Coates; by Mary Kaldor of the Armament and Disarmament Information Unit at Sussex University; by Dan Smith, a former secretary of CND whose *Defence of the Realm* had just been published; by Bruce Kent, who had just taken over as general secretary to CND; and by many others.

These others included European advisors – notably Ulrich Albrecht, Professor of Peace Studies in the Free University of West Berlin, Claude

Members of West Midlands CND demonstrate in Bonn, West Germany, 1981.

Bourdet, a lifelong compaigner and friend of CND from France, and Zhores Medvedev. The final Appeal (it is published in the Penguin edition of *Protest and Survive* and it is still an operative campaigning document) was mailed by the Russell Foundation to contacts throughout Europe (where it became in many parts known as "The Russell Appeal"). Several supporters' meetings were convened in London. At the first of these our hearts were lifted when, leaning on a stick but looking her old brisk, no-nonsense self, Peggy Duff entered the room. She had had a parting of the ways some years before with CND – in part over the issue of Vietnam – and had initiated a non-aligned peace international of which she was secretary: the International Confederation for Disarmament and Peace. When she and Bruce Kent both joined the original founding committee of END she brought with her these important international links, and the old differences which had weakened the British movement were finally buried.

The END Appeal was formally launched, with thousands of signatures from Europe as well as Britain, at the end of April 1980. My own pamphlet, *Protest and Survive*, was launched at about the same time at a press conference in CND's cellar. There commenced, for all of us, that period of active campaigning which continues to this day.

It was not then clear that CND would be the major beneficiary and organiser of this revived movement. Many of the meetings in the spring and summer of 1980 were convened by new, locally-based organisations: East Anglia Against the Missiles: the Berkshire ANC: West Yorkshire END. There were suspicions and factions around. Some ENDers suspected CND of being soft on the Soviet Union: some CNDers suspected END of dreadful things. END and CND are not identical, and although their policies complement each other, they are not the same. That their differences have contributed to variety, and strength and not to discussion has been the result of shared commitments, of the ecumenical skill of Bruce Kent, and of the facts that END renounced any intention of building a mass membership organisation in competition with that of CND. This left END with its own organisational problems which, at the time of writing, we are still trying to resolve.

END's work has been that of publication, and of communication with European movements. We have stimulated joint actions in Europe, like the demonstration in Brussels at Easter 1981, organised by a small group in West Yorkshire: put movements in touch with each other: helped British delegations to attend demonstrations at Paris, Bonn, Amsterdam, or Comiso. We have assisted with a series of conferences of peace movements: the conference convened by Peggy Duff in Frankfurt in the spring of 1981 gave important assistance to the revival, that summer, of the West German movement. The major Convention of European supporters of nuclear disarmament in Brussels in July 1982 was convened, primarily, by the Russell

Peace Foundation – which has been increasingly resuming an independent role – and with support from END.

END is a resource centre serving the British peace movement, and in close association with CND. The immense swell of European opinion for peace poses great problems of communication: monitoring, exchanges, translations. No one now supposes – as some supposed in the early days of CND – that the future will be made secure by a British "example" of morality, in renouncing our own nuclear weapons. Only a multi-national campaign, however loosely co-ordinated, will be powerful enough; and sooner or later this campaign must extend across to "the other side" also, in independent forms critical of the militarist measures of their own states. END has proposed not only common strategies to build, piece after piece, a nuclear-free Europe, but also strategies to break down the Cold War itself, to improve the flow of direct communication, and to bring movements for peace and movements for civil and trade-union rights closer to each other.

No peace movements in any two nations are alike. No national movement wants to accept the leadership of another. The Campaign against Military Bases in Iceland and No to Nuclear Weapons in Norway are alliance movements rather like CND. But in West Germany there are a multitude of movements – in the churches, among ecologists (the Greens), feminists, in the Social Democratic Party – which come together for common demonstrations. In Southern Europe the movements are even more politically-structured, and a key role is sometimes played by the Eurocommunists or by small Leftist parties. In Holland the Interchurch Peace Council (IKV) has more stability, more resources, and a greater consistency in working out strategy than any other national centre. In other countries one should speak more of a mood than a movement – a mood strongest among young people, as the CND logo spreads upon the walls of Moscow, Budapest, or Lisbon.

What END and our associated movements in Europe are doing is not only contesting nuclear weapons: we are also assisting in building the infrastructure of communication and of internationalism which is the only sound foundation for peace.

Thinking for Ourselves
Alison Whyte

In the late 1950s and early 1960s, women were active in CND in Britain and in the peace and civil rights movements in the USA. Many of these women saw the peace movement and feminism as completely separate issues and they chose to give priority to the peace movement. Some women, like Peggy Duff, were even quite sceptical of feminism.

As support for CND subsided during the later 1960s, some of the men and women who had been active in the movement put their energy into other political struggles.

> Radical politics in the 1960s provided an excellent breeding ground for feminism. Men led the marches and made the speeches and expected their female comrades to lick envelopes and listen.
>
> (Anna Coote and Beatrix Campbell in *Sweet Freedom*.)

Since the re-emergence of CND as a strong political force in this country approximately three years ago, public opinion polls have consistently shown that women are more in favour of nuclear disarmament than men. More women than men are national members of CND, and in many cases women are increasingly taking initiatives, like the Women's Peace Camp at Greenham Common, to further the cause of nuclear disarmament.

Although there is no unified women's peace movement in Britain as in some other European countries, a variety of women's groups are affiliated to CND. There are non-feminist groups like Mothers for Peace, Families Against the Bomb, and feminist groups like WONT – Women Oppose the Nuclear Threat. Many women of course are members of National CND or local CND groups but do not belong to, and may not wish to belong to, any specific women's group.

When the subject of "Women and the peace movement" is considered two issues sometimes get confused – the role of women in the peace movement and the relationship between the women's liberation movement and the peace movement.

In societies like ours, it is generally believed that women are by nature, the peaceful sex (with a few notable exceptions!). The peaceful values which are vested in women's culture have contributed to forming this myth. Women are taught to be caring, passive and non-violent. On the other hand, men are taught to be strong and aggressive and to resolve conflict with violence. Women therefore often identify with peacefulness and some see themselves as having a very distinctive role to play in the peace movement. More immediately, the reasons which many women give for being involved in the peace movement are for the sake of their children and families and to ensure that they have a future.

Those women who have not come into the peace movement through feminism in many cases have responded to the hardships which they and their children are experiencing as a direct result of an increase in military spending. As the arms race becomes more technologically sophisticated, more and more money is pumped in to maintain it. To a large extent, military expenditure dictates the rest of the Budget. Many women feel the pinch of spending on warfare not welfare directly, in reduced nursery facilities, axed school meals and low family allowances. Many women do not agree with, and reject the

Joan Ruddock, CND chairperson, speaks at the 1982 rally in Hyde Park. (*Photo:* David and Katie Urry.)

Part of the 1982 London demonstration. (Photo: David and Katie Urry.)

priorities which have been made on their behalf.

Most feminists see their feminism and their involvement in the peace movement as interrelated and would not accept that they were putting women's liberation on a shelf until later. For them, and I would include myself here, the struggle against male violence, whether on an individual level in the home or institutionalised and legitimised in the arms race, cannot be seen as separate issues. Simply calling for "equal rights" or demanding half the status quo will not do. To be hunted down in the South Atlantic by an Exocet missile, or, alongside "our boys", to blast others into an early grave, can hardly be our aim as women. Unless we challenge those values which create the mentality of the arms race, very little will have been achieved.

Some groups like WONT, because they are women-only, are seen as being separatist. In fact there is a difference between autonomy and separatism. What such groups provide is an opportunity for women to gain and maintain confidence in themselves and to work out and develop their own ideas.

Because women are largely excluded from "world affairs" their protestations are seen as being naïve, muddle-headed and idealistic, as opposed to "the mature and considered (male) view of the British public". (Paul Johnson, *Daily Mail*, 26 October 1981). It is no coincidence that this stereotypical image of women bears a striking resemblance to the image of the peace movement as depicted by the media!

A study carried out by Birmingham University's Centre for Contemporary Cultural Studies found that there was in the media "a powerful and persistent gender structuring". What is more, there has been an explosion of the language of male power and an attempt to portray the peace movement as feminine, conforming to the female stereotype in our society. The study found that behind much of the argument about the negative effects of the peace movement lurk thoroughly masculinist assumptions. "A neutral Europe would be the eunuch in the harem of great powers". (Julian Critchley, *Daily Telegraph*, 26 October 1981). The peace movement is stripped of masculinity – full of women, children, priests and long-haired youths – and embodies all the characteristics which hold no sway in our society.

Men are taught to separate heart from head – being ruled by the heart is a criticism levelled at women by men. There are two ways of talking about nuclear war. We can talk about it in terms of "first strike capability, mutual assured destruction, acceptable collateral damage". Or we can talk about it in terms of human beings dying in agony of burns and radiation sickness. Head must be reunited with heart. We must inform ourselves to the back teeth and meet the arguments of our opponents. But we must also value our feelings and have compassion.

The peace movement has much to learn from the women's movement. In this women's movement we have learned to value our own experience – to regain control over our own lives and not to allow others to make decisions on our behalf. Despite what we are taught, we cannot rely on governments or rulers to safeguard our lives and our future. We have to think and act for ourselves.

A Victory – and a New Development
Philip Bolsover

A single event in early 1980 brought home to people who had been "living with the bomb" the terrible reality of nuclear war more personally than anything that had gone before. It was the publication of the government's civil defence plans, first made known in the Home Office pamphlet *Protect and Survive.*

The fact that Cruise missiles are mobile over a radius of 100 miles and can be stationed on any well-made road brought nuclear war to the outskirts of villages in the country or suburbs in a town. But *Protect and Survive*, which sought to persuade people that they could protect themselves against bombs with the power of millions of tons of dynamite by crouching under a table, pushed the concept of nuclear war into every living-room and kitchen. Suddenly, the thing became very close, very menacing.

This pamphlet was the best gift CND ever had from any government, and the Campaign was not slow to make use of it. A reply, *Civil Defence – the Cruellest Confidence Trick*, quickly became the CND best-seller and is still selling well. Manifestly absurd proposals in *Protect and Survive* were demolished by an onslaught of criticism from many quarters; but the most damaging effect of the pamphlet (later withdrawn and re-written) was that it encouraged research into the circulars on civil defence that the government had been sending out since 1974 as instructions to local authorities, fire brigades, the police, regional health authorities and other organisations. These showed the government anticipated that during and after a nuclear attack there would be a national collapse of medical services, electricity, gas, water and food supplies. The sewage system and communications would be wrecked. A small remaining, half-starved, psychologically disturbed population, rapidly diminished by radiation sickness and ravaging epidemics, would be ruled by commissioners with dictatorial powers; and armed forces would be on hand to control looters and put dissenters into concentration camps, or in the last resort, shoot them.

This information was widely disseminated by CND, and, not surprisingly, people who had tried to ignore the danger of nuclear war found it alarming. Recruits flocked into the Campaign.

The Home Office tried to present civil defence as a humanitarian, life-saving operation, and there was a small element of truth here, but closer

examination revealed something different. Leading members of the British
Medical Association and some of Britain's most famous scientists joined CND
in declaring that civil defence would be unable to save any significant number
of people during and after a nuclear attack. Obvious conclusions could be
drawn from this. Any hopes of protecting the population were secondary;
therefore, civil defence must be for other purposes; it seemed that the most
important of these was to persuade people that they could, as individuals,
survive a nuclear war if they followed official instructions, and that such a war
was actually acceptable.

Civil defence was, in fact, a preparation for war. This was emphasised in
February 1980 by Leon Brittan, then Minister in charge of civil defence, who
told the House of Commons, according to a *Times* report, that "civil
preparedness should be adequate if the credibility of the military deterrent
strategy was to be maintained. Military and civil preparedness was closely
related".

Finally, Home Office circulars showed that the first concern of the
government was to make sure that it could control the population after an
attack; to that end it was prepared to use armed police, special courts and
internment camps.

These revelations, combined with growing alarm about the nuclear arms
race in which Britain was involved, led to one of the most remarkable
political developments of recent times – and to one of CND's greatest victories.
Following a lead from Manchester City Council, local authorities all over the
country – 140 of them at the time this book went to press – declared
themselves Nuclear Free Zones. They opposed the manufacture, deployment
or use of nuclear weapons within their boundaries, and they rejected civil
defence. Some refused to have anything whatever to do with civil defence
plans; others, including the Greater London Council, said they would fulfill
only their bare legal obligations.

Then on 14 July 1982, William Whitelaw, Home Secretary, announced that
he had been obliged to cancel the Hard Rock national civil defence exercise –
the biggest for 13 years – because conditions were inappropriate. In England
and Wales 24 of the 52 county councils had refused to participate and seven
more were co-operating only in a half-hearted way. An angry Mr Whitelaw
coupled his retreat with a threat to introduce legislation that would compel
local authorities to participate. Draft proposals for compulsion were sent out in
November 1982. When this article was written the proposals were being
strongly opposed by local authorities.

The significant thing in all this – and it was unprecedented – is that
powerful, democratically elected bodies had been convinced by CND's case
and had successfully taken direct action against the government.

CND followed up the cancellation of Hard Rock by organising an exercise

Hyde Park 1982: the poster combines opposition to nuclear power with support for nuclear-free zones.

Two demonstrators with their own views about survival. Instructions on the 'survival bags' say: "In the event of nuclear attack: place bag over head; put fingers in ears; face the other way: kiss your loved ones goodbye." (*Photo:* Pam Isherwood.)

of its own which it called Hard Luck. The basis of this was work by a specialist group of the Campaign – Scientists Against Nuclear Arms (SANA). The scientists used accurate factual information and computers to inform every locality of the effects of nuclear attack on that area – damage to buildings, the number of dead from blast, burns and radiation, each estimated separately, and other realistic information that had not been supplied to the public by the Home Office.

The civil defence campaign is a particularly fascinating part of CND's activities, deserving careful study because it shows new methods of work emerging. Traditional-style public events such as marches and demonstrations are combined with propaganda based on detailed authoritative local information and with non-violent direct action against civil defence bunkers and other installations. This is backed by what amounts in many places to a virtual partnership with the local authority, and in others a confident approach to councils and councillors.

Theresa Stewart, a Birmingham councillor, pointing to the importance of local authorities in civil defence, wrote:

> To enable a public debate to take place, and to manage the finances involved in emergency services so that they are not misappropriated towards a phoney nuclear "defence" programme, it is most important that CND demands in this area are widely discussed.

In fact, CND activities and the work of local authorities are being integrated by the civil defence campaign in a way previously unknown to CND and now highly significant.

What is this "Wider Peace Movement"?
Sheila Oakes

The rest of the peace movement has welcomed the large growth in CND over the last two years and the incredible mushrooming of local CND groups. All peace organisations are opposed to nuclear weapons, and now they all seem to support the idea that Britain should give up its nuclear weapons without waiting for international agreements – which was not true in the early days of CND

The fact that local CND groups were able to get themselves together and function so quickly was due in part to those who were already there. Think of your Quaker or pacifist members, most of whom campaign actively for nuclear disarmament and, because peace is not only a matter of disarmament, on a number of other issues as well. Peace organisations as we know them, centred around the issue of abolishing war, are a new phenomenon; most of them came into existence after the beginning of this century, and many since the 1939-45 war.

A number of people say that the peace movement is fragmented and that "what we need is a united peace movement" – envisaging, as far as I can tell, a single organisation. In my experience the peace movement *is* united: united on abolishing nuclear weapons; united on stopping the arms trade; united on the need to stop using, or depending on, "military solutions". I think it is also united in believing and urging that a greater proportion of the world's resources should go to poor people throughout the globe, and that these people should decide what are the resources that they need; and united in its belief that people as well as countries, have a right to freedom, independence and self-determination. It is not, thank goodness, united on how precisely to achieve a better sort of world, nor does it have a rigid blueprint of that better world. We are talking about futures, and these futures have not yet been tried. One of these futures is disarmament. As far as I know it has never yet happened that countries agree on voluntary disarmament; disarmament has only taken place following a war, usually by the victor disarming the vanquished.

Peace itself is a very vague concept – what do *you* mean by it? The dictionary merely says "the absence of war" but this hardly seems enough! Much of the peace movement is slowly coming to the conclusion that peace is not only an objective but also the way things are achieved – a method which cuts out conflict in the doing and does not create new conflicts for the future. There is a need for discussion, and experimentation, and a willingness to find oneself wrong – more likely partly wrong – and above all there is a need for tolerance. Being totally united must involve, at the very least, a large element of uniformity, which is death to creative ideas and creative thinking. There comes a point where I would say: "Divided we stand, united we fall!"

In the 1980s the peace movement is made up of a number of different elements. First, there are *campaigns*. These include CND, but also the Campaign Against the Arms Trade (CAAT), the Campaign Against Militarism, the Peace Tax Campaign, the World Disarmament Campaign (WDC) and others. Then there are *groups which provide some kind of service*: the Peace Advertising Campaign, the Peace Education Network, and Concord Films Council, to name but three. Then again there are *peace organisations drawn from particular constituencies*: from occupational groups such as Architects for Peace, and the Medical Association for the Prevention of War; religious groups, such as the Fellowship of Reconciliation (FOR), Quaker Peace and Service, Pax Christi, and the Anglican/Baptist/Methodist/Unitarian Peace Fellowships; and so on.

There are many groups which do not fit the categories above: the Peace Pledge Union (whose centre is pacifism). Women's International League for Peace and Freedom, East-West Peace People, and Dunamis are a few examples. And there is the peace movement's umbrella organisation, the

National Peace Council.

Peace issues do not come neatly done up in a box, or boxes, but spill over into many other issues including development, human rights, anti-racism, or ecology, and these issues spill straight back into peace issues. For this reason an individual member of CND may also be a member of, say, OXFAM, Amnesty International and/or the Anti-Apartheid Movement. Individual members will make the connections between the various, apparently separate issues, and draw the attention of other people to these connections. And nationally most of these different organisations keep each other informed as to what they are doing, and work together on specific issues or actions. For instance, a lobby of Parliament on 27 April 1982, "Disarm for Development – Lobby for Survival", was initiated by the United Nations Association, and jointly organised by them, together with Christian Aid, CAAT, World Development Movement, FoR, CND, War on Want, National Peace Council and OXFAM.

In most "western" countries the situation is similar to that in Britain. In Eastern Europe the various peace committees can best be described as "GINGOs" (Government inspired Non-Governmental Organisations). They are not directly government funded, but do not have to go out and ask individuals to contribute: they receive contributions from the people who designate the money from their "Days of Work for Socialism" to go to peace (rather than education or health for example). Their offices are provided rent-free or at a nominal rent by the local authorities. They cannot, for a variety of reasons, stray much from their own government's official policy. But, you will find, if you meet them, that the people in them do *care* very much about peace.

There are hardly any peace organisations, as such, in third world countries and even fewer independent ones.

In the space of this article it is not possible to give a detailed description of each organisation, its particular aims, objectives or services offered, or even their addresses. The best way to find out about an organisation is to ask it direct. The best single list of peace and peace-related organisations, together with their addresses and phone numbers, is in the Peace Directory section of Housman's *Peace Diary*; this diary also provides lists for other countries. You can get it from Housman's Peace Bookshop, 5 Caledonian Road, London, N1. Alternatively, the National Peace Council can send you a list of the main national peace organisations. Write to us, the National Peace Council, at 29 Great James Street, London, WC1N 3ES. Don't forget to include a stamped addressed envelope – at least! All peace organisations need money.

Why the 1980 revival happened –
and where we go from here
Joan Ruddock

CND revived because people joined. Some may remember a specific moment of decision, but for many, two years of hard campaigning will have eclipsed the memory of what exactly made them join or led them to renew a long-lapsed membership. One thing is certain – CND was not, as Frank Chapple suggested, "kissed back to life by the Kremlin"! On the contrary, Western governments provided the stimuli. NATO announced the deployment of 572 new nuclear missiles in Europe (12 December 1979) and the British government offered for sale (Spring 1980) its advice to the general public on how to prepare for a nuclear war.

Consequent on these events were many others, of which my memory highlights three. They are the House of Commons Defence debate in January 1980, revealing the Labour government's secret refurbishment of Polaris; the persuasive argument of Edward Thompson's *Protest and Survive*; and the Panorama programme of February 1980 which showed the civil defence film which the government planned to screen in the run-up to a nuclear war.

At the grass roots, some of the earliest disarmament initiatives took place around the predicted locations for Cruise missiles, Lakenheath and Upper Heyford. In both areas, broad-based campaigns were formed "Against the Missiles" – their primary aim being to stop Cruise. It is worth noting that such a revival of interest in nuclear disarmament might not have resulted in a revival of CND, had the latter not been kept in existence as a functioning entity. As it was, the philosophical and organisational base of CND had remained intact, and help was freely given to those who sought it, without any demand for allegiance.

I helped to launch an anti-Cruise group on 17 June 1980, the day the Government announced that it would allow ninety-six cruise missiles to be sited at Greenham Common. Our small Newbury group was able to respond to the considerable media interest in the base, actively contribute to what became Southern Region CND, and later provide substantial support for the women's peace camp. In common with many other groups, we campaigned for over a year before we decided to become a CND group.

Anti-Cruise campaigning was mirrored by anti-Trident as the government proceeded to unveil its plans to replace Polaris. In Scotland, supporters faced with the prospect of both American and British-owned Tridents, formed a highly successful umbrella group, Scottish Campaign Against Trident.

Recruitment drives throughout Britain were constantly fuelled by new revelations about nuclear weapons and nuclear-war planning. The publication of details of the Square Leg (civil defence) exercise by Duncan Campbell in the *New Statesman* convinced many that no place would be safe in a nuclear exchange, and that government planning envisaged the death of millions of Britons. Evidence that bunkers were being provided for an elite who planned to emerge to rule with draconian powers the sick, starving and dying, served to raise a new level of outrage against the nuclear mentality. In time, details of serious computer errors in the US nuclear-warning system, the warmongering speeches of the Reagan administration, and tensions over the Solidarity movement in Poland, all led to the fear that nuclear war was rapidly becoming inevitable. Many who had joined campaigns with more limited aims became convinced that unilateral nuclear disarmament was the only course for Britain, and our best contribution towards the growing movement for a nuclear-free Europe.

The process by which people move towards an acceptance of unilateralism, as a political goal, is worthy of analysis. My own observations suggest that the most telling arguments are those which explode the myth that nuclear weapons are solely for deterrence, and go on to show that the logical outcome of the *current* nuclear arms race is a first-strike capability. Anyone convinced by such arguments (as distinct from a moral or pacifist position) *must* advocate urgent and substantial nuclear disarmament.

The conviction that *unilateral* nuclear disarmament is the only viable option for Britain, is surely responsible for the massive increase in CND national members, in CND groups and affiliates and for the sweeping victories of unilateral nuclear disarmament resolutions at the Labour Party (1980, 1981 and 1982) and TUC (1981) conferences. So far opinion polls have still not shown a majority in favour of British unilateralism though several have shown clear majorities opposed to Cruise, to Trident and to American nuclear bases in Britain.

Clearly CND needs a strategy both to move public opinion beyond these limited goals to unilateralism and to secure implementation of that policy by government. CND strategy, such as it is, evolves from motions passed at annual conference. The 1980s have produced a campaign that looks in some ways like a re-run of the 1950s – public meetings, leafletting, petitioning and demonstrating. But those who have experienced both, note some differences. Now there appears to be a greater political realism amongst members; the "leadership" is elected from the grass roots rather than the establishment; and the 1982 annual conference enthusiastically embraced non-violent direct action as an integral part of the campaign. Slowly but surely, CND is also being influenced by the women's movement. Positive efforts are being made to support initiatives taken by women and to ensure equal representation throughout the organisation, particularly on public platforms. The importance of the youth wing of the movement is also gaining greater recognition.

Whether the new movement can be successful in securing unilateral nuclear disarmament remains to be seen. The principle of a broad-based movement was reaffirmed in 1981, and at all levels of the organisation continuing efforts are made to take the Campaign into all parts of our society.

Notwithstanding this, Conference voted to make work within the Labour movement a priority. This decision reflects the search for a means to political power. There is every reason to believe that public support can be consolidated and extended if we continue a dynamic and diverse campaign with a broad appeal; but we must also capture a government!

Valuable political experience is already accruing to CND as a result of the Nuclear Free Zones campaign. The specialist sections, Labour, Liberal and SDP CND, and the newly formed Parliamentary and Elections Committee, provide the major thrust for increasing political activity. In 1983 we are likely to see a refinement of CND's political strategy.

The success of autonomous groups such as Women for Life on Earth and Families Against the Bomb, and the very high level of activity of many CND groups begs the question, how important is the central organisation? Forty-seven thousand national CND members (in autumn 1982) provide its funding base, yet (in theory at least) it can be called upon by any of the 250,000 or so people actively supporting the movement. Personally, I am certain CND needs its central organisation, to mobilise effectively, to co-ordinate campaigns and to create a national focus to meet the challenge of the government and national media. But I have a privileged view. It takes time to develop a democracy, and National Council and its numerous sub-committees are still struggling to find effective channels of communication and decision-making. Vast sums of money are now needed to sustain the Campaign, let alone expand it, and fund *Sanity* the re-launched monthly magazine, which can be bought at commercial bookstalls.

The need for strategic thinking by CND is paramount. Opposition to our campaign is being orchestrated by Government, and pressure of time is upon us as never before. We must have a good chance of winning the battles against Cruise and Trident. But they will count for little if American bases remain in Britain and Polaris is quietly replaced by a British force of nuclear-armed Tornado aircraft. Unilateral nuclear disarmament is our goal, and in the politically decisive years of 1983/4 we must be sure of a strategy aimed at securing nothing less.

CHAPTER FIVE
A One-Issue Campaign?

Though CND's very name implies a "single-issue" campaign, different supporters are bound to interpret this in different ways. In this chapter **Hugh Jenkins**, writing from a Labour Party perspective, puts a case for keeping the Campaign's objectives extremely specific. **Howard Clark** argues that CND cannot avoid opposing nuclear energy, while **John Fremlin** puts the opposite case, saying the Campaign's present opposition is mistaken. **Dan Smith** discusses CND's possible attitude to the alternatives to a nuclear defence strategy. **Rip Bulkeley** reasserts the need for the Campaign to oppose nuclear alliances in general and British membership of NATO in particular.

A single focus
Hugh Jenkins
Opposition to the bomb is really the only thing that matters. Everything else one does and says is secondary and is carried out under the shadow of the death of civilisation.

In 1945 I was on a troopship moving into Bombay harbour when the bombs were dropped on Hiroshima and Nagasaki. I joined in the general rejoicing that the war was being brought to a rapid end (for it was some time before the truth began to penetrate) until an airman whose name I never knew said to me, "They may have saved our lives at the expense of our children's." Over the years these words grew in my mind and they have been my motivation.

I became chairman of my local Hydrogen Bomb Campaign Committee in 1954. Four years later I was on the committee which formed CND, and marched to Aldermaston, before we all realised that no one would have heard of Jesus Christ if he'd ridden *out* of Jerusalem. So after that we marched, or more often strolled, in the right direction; but we did it in a hostile atmosphere. Where today they clap, people jeered and spat at us and some towns would give us nowhere to lay our heads. That's the difference. We have turned the tide and now we are sailing with it. Shall we reach our harbour? Shall we really get rid of the Bomb at long last?

We were a powerless minority. Now we could become a powerless majority. The establishment was a powerful majority, but even if it becomes a minority, even if a unilateralist government secures office, shall we then win and lead the world into a non-nuclear age? Or will such a government be misinformed and sabotaged, politely, firmly and efficiently? This, of course, would be done in the best interests of the nation.

In a sophisticated society like ours, the people are cheated out of self-government by more complex methods than those of the brutish dictatorships which rule so many countries. Here the masses are robbed of the power to make decisions in their own interests by the skills of the con-man rather than those of the gangster. Human weakness is exploited, our tendency to be foolishly deferential at one moment and blindly aggressive the next, because we are not in charge of the events which shape our lives, is taken into consideration by those who hold the levers of authority.

CND consists of amateurs for the most part, working in our spare time. We find it difficult to sustain our effort and concentration for years on end: if we are not to become obnoxiously obsessional we have to engage ourselves in the ordinary pursuits of living. So those who lead our movement are continually changing and this has weaknesses as well as strengths.

We are constantly tempted to take our eye off the ball, to seek for short cuts, to go after the current issue. I know, because for years my own main effort was diverted on to Vietnam and into the arts, and when more recently I began to play a bigger part in CND once again, I found the bombs had trebled and deterrence had become counterforce. Then there is the temptation felt by those who do not belong to a political party, to use CND for general political purposes. Instead of the boring business of bashing on about the bomb, it can seem more satisfying both to conscience and to ego to issue a statement about Poland, El Salvador, the Falklands, Chemical Warfare, Nuclear Energy or anything else which will give us the sensation of doing something to influence the course of current events.

It is tempting but in my view it is hopelessly wrong, and it greatly pleases all the powerful enemies of nuclear disarmament to see our energies being diffused rather than concentrated on our single essential aim.

That single aim must be to get rid of the bomb from these islands. Not from Europe, not from the world – all that can come later – but from the United Kingdom. A real nuclear-free zone here, put into effect by the government of this country without consulting anyone else, is what is needed. I have been greatly concerned to hear Labour leaders, and not only Michael Foot, talking in terms of a collective European decision to denuclearise simultaneously. That means we don't get rid of our bombs until the French ditch theirs, by which time our movement may start to run out of steam again and we shall be overtaken by the holocaust.

Unilateralism means total British nuclear disarmament, including of course all American nukes, within days of taking office. Not weeks or months; let alone years, but *days*. The decision must be taken by the government and immediately put into effect, Parliament being informed simultaneously. Not asked, told. The House was not even informed when earlier decisions to nuke and re-nuke were taken. I think CND's task is to get that undertaking in unequivocal terms into Labour's General Election Manifesto and then to get Labour elected. Anything other than that, travelling about Europe, evangelising the United States, is ultimately a diversion. It may well be useful but it is not the main business in hand.

There are a lot of people spending their whole time on making sure that Britain keeps the bomb and the chances are that they will win.

The future of the world, if any, is in our hands. We must not be afraid to soil them with the grubby business of party politics. To defeat the establishment we have to become it. It is the only way.

"Civil" Energy and nuclear weapons*
Howard Clark

Campaigners for nuclear disarmament can easily become obsessed exclusively with the arms race between the superpowers. But the superpowers are not the only nuclear weapons states, and both nuclear technology and sophisticated weaponry are spreading throughout the world. Selling weapons systems and nuclear expertise is big business, a colossal waste of human resources, and it brings us nearer to war.

During the term of office of the Attlee government, while the nation was recovering from war and rationing was still in force, the government's top priority was the atom bomb programme. Never debated in parliament, this programme involved secret expenditure of £100 million, the construction of large plants and the setting up of research establishments.

The material for the first British bomb was plutonium from the first reactors (called piles) at Windscale. When demand for military plutonium increased, two nuclear power stations were ordered – Calder Hall and Chapelcross; both were to produce plutonium for weapons with electricity as a by-product. This made economic sense and also presented an opportunity for a public relations campaign about "peaceful" nuclear power. Thus, "civil" nuclear power was actually a spin off from a cover for the military nuclear programme.

After a fire in one of the Windscale piles in 1957, the piles were closed down. Since then, all Britain's nuclear weapons plutonium has been produced by reactors which also generate electricity; principally, this come from the Calder Hall and Chapelcross stations, operated by the government-owned company British Nuclear Fuels Ltd, but there is widespread suspicion that some has come from "commercial" stations run by electricity boards. One power station, Hinkley Point "A", was optimised to produce plutonium for weapons, and calculations based on questions in parliament have revealed a

* This article by Howard Clark is condensed from his CND pamphlet *Atoms For War*, published in 1982.

discrepancy of several tons between the amount of plutonium produced and the amount the government will account for (a nuclear bomb can be made with a few pounds of plutonium). The obvious implication of this is that the rest has been used for military purposes, either in Britain or traded with the US for highly enriched uranium and tritium. Highly enriched uranium is used either as nuclear submarine fuel or for nuclear weapons. Tritium is a radioactive ingredient used in H-bombs, and would also be used in neutron bombs.

By the very nature of the technology involved, the "civil" and "military" nuclear programmes are bound to have some of the same characteristics – in terms of their economies, their everyday hazards and the policing methods needed to guard such dangerous materials.

Would Britain have developed nuclear power so quickly or have become so committed to its expansion without the earlier, exclusively military, establishment of a nuclear programme? Would nuclear technology be spreading throughout the world if the giant nuclear construction industries of the West were economically viable domestically and did not actually need subsidies from either military research or export markets? "I doubt it" is my answer to both these questions.

Now, Britain is once again seeking to become more self-sufficient in its military nuclear production. One feature of this is the tritium plant which came into operation in 1980 at Chapelcross.

Nuclear proliferation

The nuclear industry's argument that no nation has used, or is likely to use, civil technology to develop nuclear weapons comes unstuck historically, politically and economically.

Historically, China apart, the first nuclear weapons states were the pioneers of nuclear electricity generation. The situation today is very different. Most of today's nuclear weapons aspirants will actually be *aided* to develop civil programmes by the more advanced nuclear states. The Indian Bomb, for instance, was made with plutonium from a research reactor supplied by Canada which was to aid India's nuclear power programme.

Politically, the argument that potential proliferators would build special weapons plants, overlooks the value of ambiguity. Most states prefer to keep their military aspirations hidden, unveiling a new weapons programme only when it is completed. Nuclear power, as well as having diplomatic advantages, has technical ones. Not only can a state order nuclear plants from abroad more easily, but it may avail itself of training programmes and advice from foreign countries. For a country undecided about whether to build nuclear weapons, embarking on a civil programme is a way of establishing a cheaper and more immediate *option* to make the weapons.

The Non-Proliferation Treaty has been signed by 110 states, but not by China or France of the official nuclear weapons states, nor by Argentina, Brazil, India, Pakistan, South Africa and Spain — all of which either can already or are near to being able to make nuclear weapons. The Treaty permits non-nuclear weapons states to proceed with nuclear development to the very brink of making a bomb and then to withdraw from the treaty at a mere three months' notice.

Never has a technology been promoted as extensively as nuclear power, despite its limited ability to meet world needs. Prof. Joseph Rotblat, deliberately calculating from assumptions that favour the nuclear industry, has shown that it will never be capable of supplying more than 10 per cent of the world's energy, and that for only a few years, because of uranium scarcity. Amory Lovins argues that economic constraints mean that nuclear electricity's contribution to world energy needs cannot exceed roughly four per cent.

Such a small return cannot justify the investment in this technology; the risks it poses — above all, the risk of a wider nuclear arms race and even more ways for nuclear wars to begin — would be calamitous if it were necessary for the world to accept them. But it isn't.

Other forms of technology have been shamefully neglected, though they promise to use energy more efficiently or to use renewable sources of energy. The world could never sustain a whole population as profligate with energy as the US, but means can be developed to harness and conserve energy to ensure enough for us all. What this requires, however, is a reversal of present priorities.

While a shift in the balance of energy research and the abandonment of pro-nuclear energy policies might slow down the spread of nuclear weapons, proliferation will not finally recede as long as "world order" and "stability" is seen to be based on the military might of competing nuclear blocs. This process has to start with the nuclear powers and the allies who play host to their weapons.

CND campaigns for unilateral nuclear disarmament by Britain to initiate wider disarmament measures. With European Nuclear Disarmament (END) and the peace movements in Europe, it also campaigns for a European Nuclear-Free Zone. The vision must not stop there, but, allying ourselves with the people of the non-nuclear countries throughout the world, we must think globally. Britain's possession of nuclear weapons adds weight to any other country's argument for an "independent deterrent".

When we have successfully refused Cruise missiles and forced the cancellation of Trident, there will still remain the sterner task of dismantling Britain's own deeply entrenched nuclear weapons production system.

Nuclear Energy; an alternative view
John Fremlin

I believe that a large majority of the British population already realise, in a non-technical but very real way, that the continued arms race is increasing rather than decreasing the risk of war starting; and I believe this majority has little else in common. To introduce extra issues is divisive, not strengthening.

If, for example, we call not merely for nuclear disarmament but for total unilateral abandonment of all forms of armament, we shall certainly please the pacifists. But they are with us already. And we should turn away a lot of people who agree with us on nuclear weapons but are genuinely afraid of giving up our conventional territorial and naval defence. So such a policy would profit us nothing, and lose an unknown but significant number of potential supporters.

A special and important case is that of civil nuclear power. Like its history in every existing sovereign country, the beginnings of this were military: the first electric-power station, Calder Hall, and perhaps the second, Chapelcross, were built for the dual purpose of producing high grade plutonium for bombs and electricity for the grid.

These two purposes are technically conflicting, not complementary. To produce electricity efficiently it is necessary to leave the uranium fuel elements in as long as possible to minimise the non-operational time. This leads the militarily useful plutonium-239 to be contaminated with large amounts of plutonium-240 which is militarily unacceptable. On the other hand, a big modern power reactor would need to be shut down about once a week to get the militarily useful plutonium efficiently; and the cost of the electricity lost would be far greater than the cost of military-grade plutonium produced in a separate reactor designed for the purpose – and the latter would have the big advantage of a staff controlled by military regulations.

Accordingly, the plutonium produced by our later Magnox stations built explicitly for electricity production, and by the AGR stations that have superceded them, is entirely unsuitable for bombs and can be efficiently used only in fast-neutron (breeder) reactors.

It is clear that, unlike the CND of the 1960s, we now have many members who are afraid of civil nuclear power. It is difficult to believe, however, that any of them regard the dangers of nuclear power as comparable to the dangers of nuclear war. Most of them seem to be thinking of the chance of such a war in the next thirty years being *at least* several per cent; while, even if the results of Rasmussen's 70-million-dollar study of the risks from one hundred nuclear power stations were optimistic by a factor of 100 (as was suggested as possible though not probable by the Kemeny Commission), the number of people expected to be killed by the hundred power stations would take about a hundred thousand years to add up to the number killed by a single A-bomb (not H-bomb).

There is only one argument which can fairly be presented in favour of opposition to nuclear power by CND. This is that the expansion of nuclear power will increase the risk of proliferation of A-bomb capacity to other countries even less responsible than the present nuclear weapon states, and hence increase the risk of world nuclear war. There is a strong case for banning the export of processing plants used to extract plutonium from spent fuel, which are far more difficult to build than are reactors; but little case against exporting the power stations themselves. It is certainly *possible* that spent fuel elements could be diverted prematurely from a power station without being reported by the IAEA inspectors. But it is also possible that this *would* be reported before the first bomb was made, with disastrous political consequences. If all processing is done by the existing nuclear weapon states, there is no need for processing plants elsewhere, and no military-grade plutonium would be available to Japan or other countries for which nuclear power may in the foreseeable future be essential to industrial survival. For this reason I believe that the opposition to the processing of Japanese spent fuel at Windscale or La Hague was seriously mistaken.

If the existing coal-rich bomb countries, such as Britain, could replace all of their coal-burning power stations by a combination of renewables (which are not yet available and cannot be used for more than 20 per cent or so of our power because of unreliability of supply), and by nuclear power (which is available), they could export the coal saved to the coal-poor countries, such as most of the Third World areas, and reduce these countries' otherwise perfectly genuine need for nuclear power. If we cannot export coal, they must have something, and it may be less dangerous to provide them with IAEA inspected nuclear power stations from outside than to drive them into building their own surreptitiously and without inspection.

The risk of an all-out nuclear war will increase if a real shortage of energy appears imminent in twenty to thirty years' time. As oil prices begin their final accelerating rise, it could become clear that whoever was in military control of the last reserves of the Middle East could be in economic control of the world. By then of course a lot more undersea sources will have been found, but these are completely vulnerable even to conventional weapons. Then the present preliminary manoevring round the Middle East – vast new US bases in North Africa, Russian occupation of Afghanistan – could become far more serious, and each side could begin to fear that the other side might be prepared to risk a limited nuclear war to get control.

I do not suppose for a moment that either side will *intend* this to happen, knowing that the ultimate escalation is almost certain to occur; but with each side doing its best to *look* as if it were serious the risk of error becomes great.

At present, misinterpretations of radar and computer malfunctions, although a genuine danger, are most unlikely to be believed by either side. Given a real strain over a real clash of vital interests, they might be believed.

The most important long-term target for peace lovers is to ensure that we do *not* have a serious shortage of energy in twenty years time. No other resource matters in comparison; given enough energy, substitutes can be produced for everything, even including natural foods.

We all hope that the renewables will be contributing usefully in twenty years' time; but nuclear power will have an essential part to play.

There are two additional points. First, the only acceptable and now available way of getting rid of our plutonium bombs is to burn them in fast neutron reactors — one such reactor can burn up to 4-5 tons of military grade plutonium. If we are serious about *complete* nuclear disarmament we must build a number of such reactors. Second, when we stop building nuclear weapons we have to do something with the huge scientific establishment at Aldermaston. It would be an excellent form of turning swords into ploughshares to put this huge stock of skilled engineers and scientists to work in the building of power stations to reduce international strain.

As with other irrelevancies, if we oppose nuclear power we please those against it who would be with us anyway — and we turn away the highly influential scientists and engineers in the peaceful power industry, many of whom will otherwise support us.

Finally, another danger of this irrelevant part of our present programme exists. The tail may wag the dog. An issue of *Sanity* a few years ago had *four times* as much material attacking nuclear power as attacking nuclear weapons. Whichever is the cause and whichever the effect, the issues of *Sanity* coinciding with the last year's splendid increase in our membership have hardly mentioned nuclear power at all.

Let us concentrate all our energies on the vitally important issue of achieving first an immediate stop to production or purchase, and then the destruction of all British nuclear weapons as quickly as is technically possible.

Alternative Defence Strategies
Dan Smith

Essentially, CND is a single-issue campaign. But the point about nuclear weapons is that there is no other single issue so imposing in its dimensions, so complex in its details and so wide-reaching in its implications and effects. Two things follow. To campaign effectively, CND has to operate at a number of different levels, addressing a wide variety of concerns. And progress towards nuclear disarmament raises a host of questions about alternative policies and perspectives.

There is no way that CND or CND activists and spokespeople can avoid addressing the questions about alternatives. The issue is raised most directly in three areas of government policy: defence, foreign affairs and social and economic priorities. But even at the level of government policy, the issue goes further than that, extending at least into questions of the direction of scientific enquiry and technological development, and into the role of the education system in either promoting or combatting a war psychology. Beyond that, further questions must be raised about the hierarchical organisation of society and social and personal relations.

However, there are ways and ways of addressing these questions. CND is not a political party, and if it starts to develop a comprehensive social and political programme to accompany its leading demand for nuclear disarmament, it will weaken its prospects for short-term partial successes and for long-term success.

One question faced by all CND activists at one time or another is, 'What defence policy do you advocate to replace our reliance on nuclear weapons?' Arising from this widely shared experience, there is a growing interest in CND developing an alternative defence policy.

I believe it would be a fundamental strategic error for CND to take this course.

To say it again, CND is not a political party. The source of our strength is our political diversity. CND is a coalition which cuts entirely through the standard divisions of party loyalty. It includes many people who in all conscience could not endorse any policy which included plans to use armed force for any purpose. And it includes many whose concern is focussed solely on the particular dimensions of nuclear weapons and nuclear war.

Moreover, the fact that CND is not a political party means it cannot aspire to hold governmental power. Political parties which aspire to form a government need to have defence policies, and CND's role is to do everything it can to form a climate of opinion in which the defence policies developed by parties are non-nuclear, and in which the electorate opts for a party or parties with non-nuclear defence policies.

In other words, CND's basic role is to close the door against certain options in defence policy – nuclear options. Since it will never have to implement a defence policy it is needless and inappropriate for it to develop one.

However, CND can and should show that there is a range of alternatives: the idea that there could be an alternative to the way things are now done is an important and powerful idea, and it will help the cause of nuclear disarmament if that idea is developed, specified and publicised.

There are numerous possibilities, ranging from planning for non-violent resistance to aggression and conquest, through various models of guerrilla-style territorial defence, to orthodox but non-nuclear conceptions of the role and organisation of armed forces, and there are combinations of all three.

Thus one can conceive of a defence policy in which orthodox armed forces are utilised, but in which changes have been made to reduce the reliance on major weapon systems of huge sophistication and massive cost. Such forces could be supplemented or replaced by preparations for regular military or citizens; militia forces to harass and destroy the aggressors' forces. Non-violent resistance could be regarded as the line of last defence, to make conquest and sustained occupation impossible; or its potential as the main form of defence could be explored further.

Similarly, defence preparations of these kinds by Britain could be attached to a concept of independent defence in which Britain had pulled out of NATO, or could be linked to continued membership of NATO and an effort to "de-nuclearise" NATO's military stance, at least in Europe.

Choices between these alternatives would reflect both basic political principles and a political calculation as to the best way of achieving British and European nuclear disarmament.

I have not simply plucked these alternatives out of the sky. There is a rich and growing literature on the possibilities for defence policy without nuclear weapons. The Alternative Defence Commission, established by the Bradford School of Peace Studies and the Lansbury Trust, is one forum in which this literature has been brought together and surveyed. To promote alternative conceptions of defence — to promote the consciousness that there could be alternatives — all CND need do is point people in the direction of the most accessible and readable of this literature. Local CND groups and other organisations can easily set up study groups to study alternative defence strategies so that activists are better able to answer that tricky question, "What is the alternative?" To do all of this, it is not necessary for CND formally to endorse one alternative as against any other.

Two basic assumptions should perhaps guide us as we think about alternatives. The first is the recognition that as a way of providing genuine security, armed force is far from the most important or effective instrument, and that it has proven to be an uncomfortably two-edged sword. The second is the recognition that Britain does not now have a policy that provides security or is designed for defence. Faced with the question, "What do you think about British defence policy?" our most appropriate answer is perhaps the same as Gandhi's, when he was asked what he thought about Western civilisation. He replied, "I think it would be a good idea."

Nuclear Allies? No Thanks!
Rip Bulkeley

"Here's the writing on the wall,/This is what is written:/Boot the bases, ban the bomb,/And up with neutral Britain." The chorus of an old CND song lists three aspects to unilateralism, our short-term programme for freeing Britain from complicity in the Cold War and the nuclear arms race, though not initially from their fearful dangers. This three-fold unilateralism has been fundamental to CND since 1960, when our policy that Britain should unilaterally walk out of NATO was first decided. And it stands today in the first paragraph of CND's Constitution:

> The aim of CND is the unilateral abandonment by Britain of nuclear weapons, nuclear bases *and nuclear alliances* as a prerequisite for a British foreign policy which … etc [emphasis added].

(Before going on, one word about that puzzling plural "nuclear alliances". When written it referred to NATO plus two other anti-Soviet military pacts, CENTO and SEATO, that Britain had been roped into as junior partner by the United States, but which have since collapsed. CND's wisdom in seeing the other two as also potentially nuclear was shown when the Wilson govenment sent nuclear V-bombers to Singapore five years later. The demise of SEATO and CENTO mean that the Constitution should, strictly, be updated by changing "nuclear alliances" to read simply "NATO", and I shall take it that way in what follows.)

The main reason for CND wanting Britain out of NATO is simple consistency. The many and various arguments against nuclear weapons almost all apply with the same force against letting them be deployed somewhere else "on our behalf" by another government, as they do against having them in Britain. And the importance of being consistent about our refusal of so-called nuclear defences is made clear by the eagerness of CND's opponents to trap us into saying we want a free ride, that is, to shelter under an American nuclear umbrella while refusing to accept our nuclear responsibilities to Britain's allies. The only answer must be that we want no part of any such thing, and that our over-riding responsibility to the people of the countries referred to is to help them undermine the nuclear madness of their rulers as quickly as possible.

It is anyway very unlikely that such a hypocritical option would be available to Britain, even if we did want it. British unilateral nuclear disarmament will mean major political and military disruption for NATO, because Britain just is not the military, political or geographical equivalent of Canada, whose rejection of offensive (but not defensive) nuclear hardware has passed off relatively smoothly. The knock-on effects of British unilateralism will be so devastating, in the present state of NATO, that if a recognisable nuclear NATO survived, Britain would not be welcome in it.

It would obviously be foolish to expect worldwide nuclear disarmament to happen at the same instant as the local British variety. Instead, there will go on being a nuclear confrontation between the rulers of the two superpowers, whether escalating or, hopefully, de-escalating under pressure from world opinion. Militarily senseless and humanly sickening as this fact may be, there are motives of imperialist "face", the ghastly semantics of the arms race, why it will be so. Therefore Britain cannot just opt out of the nuclear aspect of the Cold War — any version of the Atlantic Alliance, no matter what its official strategy or disposition of nuclear weapons, will be nuclear for as long as the United States remains so. (A European Defence Community, with Western Europe opting out of the American nuclear protection racket in favour of some non-nuclear military arrangements of its own, would perhaps be another matter.)

It follows that neutrality, in the sense of a Europe-oriented anti-nuclear foreign policy, is what CND should continue to propose for a Britain freed from nuclear weapons. The whole point of unilateralism being, as the sentence from the Constitution already quoted ends

> ... as a prerequisite for a British foreign policy which has the worldwide abolition of nuclear, chemical and biological weapons leading to general disarmament as its prime objective.

Indeed, the relative lack of impact of Canada's unilateral nuclear disarmament has been a corollary of her failure to take the next important step, out of NATO. We should be warned by this example.

But support for CND's opposition to NATO is *relatively* weaker than for our other policies, even inside the Campaign. In part this is a natural result of the new movement's preoccupation with immediate issues such as Cruise Missiles. It is also due to our recent rapid growth, in which tens of thousands of people have rushed into CND out of fear and indignation at the escalating arms race, but without always informing themselves fully of CND's stated political aims, or thinking through the political implications of unilateralism in the real world.

Another reason may be the very fact that CND is now closer than ever before to achieving its objectives. An organisation can often develop a certain timidity or nervousness about its own long-held views, as the moment for putting them into practice approaches. The more so as we face a storm of vituperation from opponents, who emphasise the stupid charge of "treason" as hard as possible. Part of this hesitation has been the claim that our policy of leaving NATO is unrealistic, and the Labour Party in particular will never accept it. This ignores the significant growth of the anti-NATO vote between the 1980 and 1981 Labour conferences, even though CND has done nothing lately to canvass support for the policy.

As for realism, if, as experts on both sides of the disarmament debate believe, unilateralism effectively implies British departure from NATO (or else NATO's collapse), then CND is right to have the guts and honesty to say so, especially since the public always raises this question with us.

The current debate about NATO in CND starts from an important difference between our situation today and twenty years ago. Since we are now part of a loose federation of West European nuclear disarmament movements, some people want our NATO policy to be worked out as a consensus with them, dropping the idea of a lone British walk-out. But the conclusion doesn't really follow. If it did, the same argument would prove we should also give up the present friendly race to see which national movement can unilaterally slam the door in the face of Cruise Missiles the soonest. Whereas in fact any one country's unilateral refusal of either a part or the whole of nuclear NATO will be an enormous boost to similar campaigns all over Europe, East and West. Besides which, historic national differences between the various movements mean that a proposal to "wait until we all agree" amounts to putting the whole thing off to "the twelfth of Never", exactly the sort of procrastination we condemn in our opponents.

The latest surge in the superpower arms race, and the wave of popular opposition to it, face CND with an urgency and an opportunity such as it has never had to live up to before. This is no time for faint-hearted etiquette in front of the NATO Exit door about who leaves first, or whether countries should leave one at a time or arm in arm. All that is needed is a determination that whichever movement first makes it out into anti-nuclear freedom will turn round and widen the breach for friends still trapped inside a senseless nuclear alliance.

CHAPTER SIX
Words, music and marches

Four writers were asked for personal recollections that reflected the style of the movement over its first fifteen years, and the music, songs and plays, written and spoken words, that helped to shape CND. **Adrian Henri** includes episodes from the early Aldermaston marches to the Campaign's festivals for peace in the early 1970s. **Ian Campbell** recalls how jazz and folksong became part of the movement's style for many years. **Peter Worsley** looks at the results of the unprecedented political mixture that made up CND; and **Adrian Mitchell** indicates some of the books, plays, films and poems that have nourished the peace movement. "On the Beach at Cambridge" is his own recent contribution.

It seemed right, and still does
Adrian Henri

> Aldermaston dogs scowling through wire at happy marchers
> banners black-and-white against Falcon Field
> proud trumpet breaking out over the marching drums
> the uphill road   tired legs   feet sore
> Joyce and I with the huge wurst sausage
> we took every year to eat at roadsides
> thrown into horseboxes by grinning policemen on demos.
>
> from *Autobiography* (1970)

1

My experience of Aldermaston marches was a strange one: from foot-soldier in Russell's army to general — or at least ENSA entertainer.

Though born on Merseyside I'd been brought up in Rhyl, North Wales. Every summer that I was short of money I'd go back to work in the fairground. One day a schoolboy called Mike Evans saw a Chet Baker record on the back of my burst-a-balloon stall, got talking, and became a lifelong friend. His passions were jazz, blues and CND. I didn't have any particular contact with Liverpool CND groups at the time, which is how I came to march every year under the banner of RHYL YOUTH with Evans and his mates, although nearly thirty. My confused memories of different years run into each other, as in the bit of the long poem quoted above. Sore feet, the blankets off our beds rather than sleeping bags, hard schoolroom floors, my wife and I buying a whole kosher salami to eat with bread brought along the way. One unforgettable moment: someone playing a march-rhythm up ahead on a snare-drum, then, as the column moved up the hill, a trumpet suddenly breaking out into the Miles Davis solo on "Gone" from *Porgy and Bess* against the drum-beat. Familiar faces: Richard Hamilton, who'd taught me at college, at the side of the road with a life-size cut-out Marilyn holding a CND lollipop. David Hockney, gleaming blond hair, red-and-white striped jacket. George Melly and Simon Watson Taylor, Simon with a walking-stick incorporating a flask "in case he got arrested". Going off on the next-to-last night to see The Living Theatre in *The Connection* with Jackie McLean playing alto sax on stage. Pete Brown dashing about in his On-The-Road outfit organising parties. Strange ritual of friends met once a year at the roadside. Buying my first copy of *Freedom*. And the songs: "The H-Bomb's Thunder" and "The Family of Man". Wild-looking Scots singing "We are The Glasgow Eskimos".

Joyce and I arrested on Committee of 100 demos in Manchester and Liverpool: me always last because they kept avoiding carrying the heavy ones. I had a plan for an elite corps of overweight demonstrators to sit at the front and tire out the police. And we pinned the "Spies for Peace" leaflet to the front door of our basement flat in Falkner Square.

A: Get PAD nuclear meat for humans

B: Don't give your family ordinary meat, give them PAD.

A: P-A-D Prolongs Active Death.

B: Enriched with nourishing, marrowbone strontium.

from *Bomb Commercials*

From a set of commercials I wrote for a Happening called *Bomb*, performed at the Cavern, Liverpool in 1965. I still read them at gigs today: they're sadly all too topical. This was a multi-media anti-nuclear extravaganza with The Clayton Squares, best of the post-Beatles groups, including Mike Evans on saxophone. He'd dropped out of studying sociology, fallen for a Liverpool girl, come here with his sax and joined a band. There was a vocal group (later to find fame as Arrival), Bob Wooller, the legendary Cavern DJ, and a host of others.

At the end of a four-minute countdown the lights went out and a false ceiling made of paper came down on peoples' heads, to the most deafening noise we could devise. The cloakroom girls screamed and hid under the counter. In the darkness and confusion, strange mutant figures moved.

Sitting on a train.
Wondering will daffodils and rhododendrons stand against the cruel bayonets?
Will telling my love for you change the Universe?

Will telling you walking to school in winter morning darkness
Cold in your brown uniform
Keep the Napalm from one frightened child?

from "Spring Song for Mary"

1969 been and gone, I've changed from art teacher to bestselling poet to poet/singer with "The Liverpool Scene", a berserk poetry/folk/rock'n'roll group. Mike Evans plays saxophone and does songs and poems. Andy Roberts on guitar, Percy Jones, now of Brand X, on bass, Pete Clark on drums.

It's 1970 and we're doing an outdoor concert for CND at Victoria Park, Hackney. For some reason we had recently been "adopted" by Crazy Dog, a pack of Hell's Angels from Bishops Stortford. Everywhere we went round London, there they were. Nazi helmets, colours, the lot. This time, as usual, they got up on stage with us and danced to our last few numbers, notably "Baby", a poem turned anti-Enoch rock'n'roll diatribe. Being preoccupied with leaping about the rather shaky temporary stage, I hadn't noticed that a huge gang of skinheads, the Angels' natural enemies, had turned up and were pelting them (and us) with bottles and beercans. I did wonder why Andy and Percy were playing *behind* their amplifiers, though. How brave I was to face up to them, everyone said later.

Give peace a chance.
Give peace a chance
Let the whole world learn to Rock'n'Roll"

Delaney & Bonney Bramlett,
"Give Peace a Chance"

The band broke up in Summer 1970. After that I was part of a collection of touring lunatics called Grimms, and led numerous put-together-by-telephone groups called Henri and Friends. From a number of CND occasions through that period I recall best a huge concert at Alexandra Park in 1971, and a rally on Falcon Field, Aldermaston, in 1972 (infantry-man becomes entertainer for the troops). On the first occasion I was with Alan Peters (trumpet, guitar, vocals), Dave Richards (bass) and Andy. We did, amongst other things, Dave's song "We Are The Police", part of the chorus of which goes:

And we will fight for your right to die like pigs
In the next a-tomic war ...

and ending up with Delaney and Bonney's classic peace anthem, with thousands of voices joining in at the end. Wonderful. Peel was there, Frances my then-new girlfriend, Mike Hart got up and sang with us.

The other occasion I remember chiefly for my last sight of poor dead Graham Bond, for my money the only Englishman who's ever played the blues like a black American. Leaping about in a black wizard costume as part of "Bond and Brown", with Pete Brown who'd written the lyrics for Cream and led a string of bands of his own since those early marching, hitch-hiking poet days. Reading on my own this time, along with brother poet Adrian Mitchell.

Why, I wonder reading through all this, did it seem so natural for poets and jazzmen and rock'n'rollers to put their services at the disposal of the peace movement? It seemed right at the time, and still does. All artists work in the dark, alone. Perhaps, for a few days or hours every year, we didn't feel so alone because we were part of something bigger.

Music Against the Bomb
Ian Campbell

In the 1950s teenagers had hardly been invented. The seeds of today's diverse harvest were only being sown and counter-cultures were unobtrusive. Still scarred by National Service army conditioning we tended to sport short-back-and-sides haircuts with sports coat and flannels; the jeans fad had not yet flourished; neither had the pop industry as we know it today. Records presented orchestra and dance bands who usually featured a resident vocalist singing songs from stage shows or films, or speciality numbers produced to meet band needs by the Tin-Pan Alley industry. Apart from the odd novelty, such as a tongue twister or comic song in the music hall tradition, songs were invariably about love, or rather a peculiarly wholesome and sexless variety of romance.

Having no access to any process by which we could influence popular music, many of us turned our backs on it and looked elsewhere for musical pleasure. We found an underground movement among musicians, a music played by amateurs and by professionals in their spare time, in private clubs and in pub backrooms; it throbbed with life and a spirit of independence, its syncopated rhythms were an affront to the conventions of ballroom dancing, and the words of the songs dealt with unprecedented subjects like work, drink, the sex war, abortion, racial discrimination – all the domestic pleasures! It was trad jazz.

It is significant that 1958, the year that saw the climactic boom in jazz popularity, also produced the first Aldermaston march. The jazz revival and the rise of CND were more than coincidental; they were almost two sides of the same coin. Similar social attitudes and positive humanist values informed them both. At any jazz event a liberal sprinkling of CND badges, and perhaps even leaflets and posters, would be in evidence; conversely, at every CND demonstration live jazz music set the tempo for the march.

At one of the Easter rallies in the early 1960s I stood and watched for a while as over 100,000 demonstrators – several miles of them – marched into Hyde Park. CND was then, as again now, at its broadest as a popular movement, and among the students, pensioners and pram-pushing housewives were organised groups from trades unions, political parties, churches, youth movements and so on; every hundred yards or so there was a group of musicians – some of them rare and wonderful combinations, such as a bagpipe-tuba duo or a children's kazoo and percussion band – but predominantly they were jazz combos, and I lost count of the versions I heard of "Down by the Riverside" and "The Saints Go Marching In".

In the mid-Fifties the jazz revival had produced an offshoot, a musical phenomenon which became much bigger than itself, the skiffle craze. Skiffle was do-it-yourself music, primitive jazz played on home-made or improvised rhythm instruments as an accompaniment to the singing of folk-blues and jazz songs of the simpler and more repetitive sort. Much of its appeal was that the performers required no musical training or skill apart from a basic sense of rhythm and three chords on the guitar.

When in 1956 Christ Barber's banjoist, Lonnie Donegan, put a skiffle record into the charts the craze took off; for a couple of years the nation fell for the three chord trick and cheap guitars were made and sold in unprecedented numbers. When commercial over-exploitation killed the craze thousands of budding guitarists were left all geared up with nowhere to go; many of them lengthened their straps to go into Rock and Rhythm and Blues, and Furied and Stormed their way toward Beatle- and Stonedom; others went back into the pubs and started the British folksong revival.

Just as in the Fifties the rise of CND coincided with the jazz boom, so in the Sixties the great flowering of the peace movement went hand in hand with the folksong revival. Already on the first Aldermaston march were folksong enthusiasts like John Brunner, who utilised the tune of an American folksong when he wrote the first great CND anthem "The H-Bombs' Thunder".

As anthems necessarily are this is a simple straightforward song: sometimes Campaigners tend to sing it, like Labour parliamentarians singing "The Red Flag", with an air of slight embarrassment. It would be difficult, however, to overestimate its value to CND during the Sixties, particularly on the big demos. It was uniquely effective in generating a proud sense of unity and identity among the demonstrators; its slightly hymnal folktune was easily learnt and suitable for jazz band performance, and its strong rhythm made it an ideal marching song.

As the folksong movement burgeoned and clubs opened all over the land they more than filled the place left by the shrinking jazz movement. The folk clubs became the places where duffle-coat lapels flaunted CND badges and anti-war songs were assured a sympathetic reception. There are many anti-war songs in the folk tradition, and the theme was popular in the clubs. An inevitable development was that singer/songwriters started to produce contemporary songs on the same theme. The Glasgow Eskimos, Scottish folksingers active in the campaign against Polaris in the Holy Loch, created a whole genre of satirical dialect songs; Ewan MacColl and the Critics Group spearheaded a movement in writing songs of political and social comment; the Vietnam war backlash produced writers in the US as varied as Tom Lehrer and Tom Paxton whose songs were known and valued here, but even earlier British writers like Leon Rosselson and Sydney Carter had produced innumerable peace songs to complement if not replace "The H-Bombs' Thunder".

The warm fraternity of the peace and folk movements, and the ready demand for peace songs in the folk clubs, was illustrated for me by a remarkable incident which also showed the surprising speed with which songs could still be passed on by word of mouth today, in the twentieth century. In 1961 I wrote an anti-war song called "The Sun is Burning", and before it had been published or recorded my sister Lorna performed it publicly for the first time one Saturday at the London Ballads and Blues Club. On the following Tuesday at our own Jug o' Punch Club in Birmingham a visiting singer sang it to us, introducing it as a new song he had learnt at a Bristol CND event that weekend. I am glad to say the song has lasted well and was in the Irish charts during 1981.

Although neither jazz nor folksong is booming at the moment, there is no reason to fear that peace songs will cease to be written and performed. Among the many factions in musical subculture are now plenty who include war among the objects of their invective, and the message of peace is heard more widely than ever. Right on, kids. Write on.

Political Culture, Political Style
Peter Worsley

In her book *Left, Left, Left*, Peggy Duff, the beating heart of CND in the Sixties, quotes Freda Ehlers, a Bristol Campaigner, who lamented: "In CND, I have to mix with so many odd people that the sooner we ban the Bomb the better."

CND was a *movement*, not a party. It brought together people from very diverse political, social and religious backgrounds: the activists on the march were the "middle-class radicals" Frank Parkin wrote about, only 4 per cent of them recognisably working-class, according to a 1959 survey. Labour MPs and *New Statesman* figures had played a major role in starting the Campaign, and the battle was to reach its climax within the Labour Party once unilateralism had become a force in the trade unions. But most of the membership were liberal-minded Labour voters who had, however, never been involved in politics before, even though they regarded themselves as "political".

With an influence out of all proportion to their numbers were the pacifists, of various kinds. What I remember most vividly about the coast-to-coast march of 1958 (apart from dropping out crippled near Manchester) was arguing for hours, on the road, with not just a pacifist, but an ultra-pacifist vegan called Carol about the ethics of killing and eating animals. So some of us even seemed "weird" to each other, not just to opponents ready to write us all off as deviants. Pacifists and vegetarians were people that ex-Communist New-Lefters like myself had never run across before. To my surprise, they were often not at all gentle or disposed to turn the other cheek. They were activists and radicals ready to do things much more daring and serious in their personal consequences than us, for all our revolutionism.

Indeed it was their influence, I believe, that injected into a movement largely composed of Labour supporters and a Left thoroughly steeped in parliamentarism and "respectable" tactics, an intransigent militancy that the Left lacked: not petitions and processions, but sit-downs and "direct" action.

And CND was a movement of *young* people. Today, we forget that at the beginning of the 'sixties we in the New Left still found it necessary to write a book called *Out of Apathy*, for apathy had been the condition of the young until the double crisis of Suez and Hungary exposed both Western imperialism and Soviet repression.

This mixture of elements was bound to produce some novel syntheses – and did. One significant novel influence was our New Left. "More than any other element in the politics of unilateralism", Christopher Driver has written (*The Disarmers* p. 73), "this group belonged to its time". It was the pioneer of the argument for non-alignment and positive neutralism – the predecessors of the nuclear-free zone campaign.

The spectrum from Left Labour MP to radical pacifist was so wide that new sub-groupings kept constantly emerging, all under the umbrella of CND, but with very distinctive styles of their own. Yet there was an overall style, the new public face of a distinctive political culture, the feel and sight of which excited those who were part of it and disturbed their opponents. Above all, it was *public*: people who would have previously been horrified even to think of walking in the gutter, holding placards, or marching down the middle of the road in their shopping-centre, proclaiming their beliefs, found it hard. It involved a departure from conventional norms of respectable behaviour that some found painful; mild, certainly, in comparison with sacrificing one's life or livelihood, but involving a degree of readiness to risk being labelled "nutty" or stupid, even ostracised by the neighbours if need be. It was in the small local groups where the real work of "campaigning" was done.

Aldermaston, of course, was the high point, full of excitement and colour, banners and badges. Exhibitionists were in their element, and Press and TV homed in on them as an easy way of writing off the duller 98 per cent as "weirdies" as well, however conventional their hair or dress. Yet in a much less sensationalist sense, the movement *was* unorthodox, and many were soon to be pushed into doing much more unorthodox things – things they would never have contemplated a couple of years earlier. They were even brought up against the prospect of prison – but prison terms they were to invite by conscientiously breaking the law.

In 1961 the Labour Party reversed its 1960 decision to support CND policy. For many, it was the end of orthodox politics, especially among that majority of CNDers who had never been involved with any of the established parties – and nine out of ten of the young people on the 1959 survey of the Aldermaston marchers supported the Campaign for moral reasons. Blocked on the political front, and spurred by the desperate conviction that we were on the edge of destruction, protest was now directed not just against the Bomb, but against a political system whose managers had been able to hang on to power despite defeat. Their control of the political machinery had been critical. But they had also been able to retain the support of the majority of people in the country, even between March 1959 and April 1960, when over 30 per cent declared support for unilateralism in opinion polls.

Radical pacifists, with long experience of non-violent resistance, were able to provide a variety of models and tactics quite unfamiliar to either the electoral or the revolutionary Left, beginning with symbolic "sit-downs", then independent election campaigns, through to the blocking of military sites and the exposure of the existence of top-secret regional seats of government. Embarrassed, even hostile at first, CND National Executive came to recognise the impact of these tactics, and the right of those who used them to do so, without directly supporting them.

We awoke at the beginning of the 1980s to a new realisation of the greatest danger in human history. Annual marches may have become an expressive ritual of solidarity, absorbing too much energy, and diverting us from the mundane central job of changing other people's minds: a symbol of our status as a minority relating to each other, rather than a movement whose first priority has to be those who don't – at present – agree with us.

Yet the marches of our early years expressed that very simple, fundamental realisation that there is no way we can save our own lives as individuals and communities, except by halting the steady drift of the entire world to destruction. That involves mobilising people who come from all parties and none: and today, in CND we seem to be reaching out in new ways to more people than ever before, even in the heady days of the early 1960s.

The visions of many artists
Adrian Mitchell

Part of my generation's hatred for war dates back to pre-bomb days, indeed to the First World War in which my mother lost both her brothers, and my father – four years in the trenches – lost nearly all his friends. The images of that war were very strong in my mind as a teenager. *All Quiet On The Western Front*, Wilfred Owen, Siegfried Sassoon and Isaac Rosenberg's poems. Their images of the Western Front as a wasteland, a dead planet, seeped into my mind and so, when it came to imagining the Third World War, it was a matter of envisaging whole continents as the Western Front, with those dead, broken trees, waterfilled craters, the dead and the mud indistinguishable from each other.

A few of the playwrights of the fifties attacked the matter of war or peace, but very few. Those were the days of censorship in theatre. Arden's *Sergeant Musgrave's Dance* grew out of atrocities in Cyprus, but its reverberations stretched into the future. There was a play (and film) by the late Roger MacDougall called *Escapade* about a schoolboy who flew on a peace mission because he couldn't stand the possibilities of extinction. There was, above all, Samuel Beckett's *Endgame*, which provided a very realistic vision of the last days of the planet.

Then there are movies: *Orders To Kill* (Asquith, script by Paul Dehn), was ostensibly about World War II. Its plot concerns a young pilot who finds it easy to drop bombs which kill a hundred people, but finds it horrific and traumatic when he has to make friends with a traitor, and then stab him to death, messily, with scissors. The film exposes the lack of imagination which makes it possible to kill people you never saw and can believe are ogres or slaves (like the men, women and children of Russia). *The War Game* is obviously of great importance, but so is Peter Watkins's *Culloden* which is also about the obscenity of slaughter. I thought *Failsafe* was a bit dead because I wasn't interested in the people, but Stanley Kubrick's *Doctor Strangelove* I think a fine and important piece of work. Fight madness with jokes.

Newsreels of Nagasaki and Hiroshima in various compilation movies have been essential to anyone who begins to imagine the bomb.

I find that often, when I can bear them, pro-war movies, etc. rouse me into action. Like the bloody *Dam Busters*, one of the vilest movies ever made. Or *Blood on the Sun* in which the Japanese are branded as total monsters. Or, for that matter, all these ultra-violent *Car Death Race Rollerball Chainsaw Halloweens* in which terror and sadism are glorified, and bored little critics applaud the thrills they can only get from "exploitation movies".

Among novels, *Level Seven* by Mordecai Roshwald is gruelling and true. Kurt Vonnegut's *Slaughterhouse Five* and *Cat's Cradle* are valuable; and I especially admire Peter C. Brown's masterpiece, *Smallcreep's Day*, which is not only a condemnation of the Bomb but also of the civilisation which produced it. I guess Neville Shute's *On The Beach* has been influential, but I never read it or saw the movie.

Many poets have written specifically about World War III – Denise Levertov, Kenneth Patchen, Kenneth Rexroth, Allen Ginsberg in the USA, Roy Fisher, Christopher Logue and Ted Hughes over here.

Robert Jungk's *Brighter than a Thousand Sons* and *Children of the Ashes* are essential. So is E.P. Thompson's *Protest and Survive*, to be read in conjunction with HMSO's *Protect and Survive*. So, in other ways, are Jeff Nuttall's *Bomb Culture* and Peter Laurie's *Beneath the City Streets*. We need many more books, plays, movies, TV programmes, songs and poems about the future of our planet. No single artist can supply a total vision of the probably horrific future. But the visions of many artists are cumulative.

Goya's *Horrors of War* plus Theatre Workshop's *Oh, What a Lovely War*! plus *Les Jeux Interdits* plus *King Lear* plus Raymond Briggs' *When The Wind Blows* plus the poems of Heathcote Williams and Nicki Jackowska plus the graphic works of Ralph Steadman may seem an unlikely sum. But they add up and, for me, they add to the energy with which I hope to struggle, alongside you, for the survival of the planet and, one day, for Peace.

On the Beach at Cambridge

I am Assistant to the Regional Commissioner
At Block E, Brooklands Avenue,
Communications Centre for Region 4,
Which used to be East Anglia.

I published several poems as a young man
But later found I could not meet my own high standards
So tore up all my poems and stopped writing.
(I stopped painting at eight and singing at five).
I was seconded to Block E
From the Ministry for the Environment.

Since there are no established poets available
I have come out here in my MPC,
(Maximum Protective Clothing),
To dictate some sort of poem or word-picture
Into a miniature cassette recorder.

When I first stepped out of Block E on to this beach
I could not record any words at all.
So I chewed two of the orange-flavoured pills
They give us for morale, switched on my Sony
And recorded this:

I am standing on the beach at Cambridge.
I can see a group in their MPC
Pushing Hoover-like and Ewbank-like machines
Through masses of black ashes.
The taller men are soldiers or police,
The others, scientific supervisors.
This group moves slowly across what seems
Like an endless car park with no cars at all.

I think that, in one moment,
All the books in Cambridge
Leapt off their shelves,
Spread their wings
And became white flames
And then black ash.
And I am standing on the beach at Cambridge.

You're a poet, said the Regional Commissioner,
Go out and describe that lot.

The University Library — a little hill of brick-dust.
King's College Chapel — a dune of stone-dust.
The sea is coming closer and closer.

The clouds are edged with green.
They are sagging low under some terrible weight.
They move more rapidly than usual.

Some younger women with important jobs
Were admitted to Block E
But my wife was a teacher in her forties.
We talked it over
When the nature of the crisis became apparent.
We agreed someone had to carry on.
That day I kissed her goodbye as I did every day

At the door of our house in Chesterton Road.
I kissed my son and my daughter goodbye.
I drove to Block E beside Hobson's Brook.
I felt like a piece of paper
Being torn in half.

And I am standing on the beach at Cambridge.
Some of the men in their MPC
Are sitting on the ground in the black ashes.
One is holding his head in both his hands.

I was forty-two three weeks ago.
My children painted me
Bright-coloured cards with poems for my birthday.
I stuck them with Blue-tack on the kitchen door.
I can remember the colours.

But in one moment all the children in Cambridge
Spread their wings
And became white flames
And then black ash.

And the children of America, I suppose.
And the children of Russia, I suppose.

And I am standing on the beach at Cambridge
And I am watching the broad black ocean tide
Bearing on its shoulders a burden of black ashes.

And I am listening to the last words of the sea
As it beats its head against the dying land.

Adrian Mitchell
Cambridge, March 1981

CHAPTER SEVEN
Many allies – and we need them all

Contributors here discuss how the Campaign should relate to a number of bodies where CND has widespread, but not automatic, support; they are, with one exception, CND members who play an active part in the organisations they discuss. **Andrew Papworth** writes of CND's relationship to Britain's political system from a position *outside* partly politics. **Paul Oestreicher** considers how CND can appeal to churches on the basis of their own faith and position. **Ruth Longoni** and **Walter Wolfgang** discuss the involvement of trade unionists in the Campaign. **David Griffiths** surveys areas of interaction with the Labour Party. **Isobel Lindsay** outlines the strong Scottish and Welsh nationalist opposition to nuclear military policies; and **Robert Fyson** identifies some points of contact with the Liberal-SDP Alliance.

CND and Party Politics: a view from the outside
Andrew Papworth

Is there a real chance that we might do something effective about the prospects of mass destruction? How do we view the prospects of success for the nuclear disarmament movement? And what series of political steps do we envisage as a potential route to the realisation of our demands, at least as far as Britain is concerned? In seeking answers we can look at the movement of the late fifties and early sixties. I return to the sixties only because there did seem to be some real optimism around then that the movement might be capable of achieving some of its demands.

It is difficult to describe the earlier movement as a success or a failure: it was both. A brief evaluation of it is given in the introduction to this book. Here I simply want to stress my view that it was a major success in terms of the widespread support that it mobilised, involving so many people that it left many marks on British society; and that it was a substantial failure in having virtually no effect on government disarmament policy, in spite of partial successes like the 1963 Test Ban Treaty. I think the movement declined chiefly because real success seemed as distant as ever, and movement activists began to feel powerless to achieve their goals. They despaired precisely because of the contrast between its success in mobilising so many people and the refusal of the political system to take heed of them. I suggest that CND became, for many thousands that were drawn into it, a test of Britain as a democracy and that it failed the test.

CND began with a favourable view of the British political system. It believed the system was sufficiently democratic and open to persuasion to reponds to what CND's first chairperson, Canon collins, described as a "sharp, virile and successful campaign". This favourable view was linked with patriotism: Milton's injunction "Let not England forget her precedence in teaching the nations how to live" was a popular quotation for speakers. The key point for us now is that we did not then appreciate the radical nature of our unilateralist demand, nor the nature of the political system.

A whole series of experiences was to indicate to many of us that the system was not democratic, nor amenable to the kind of changes we were seeking. There was the realisation, rather late in the day, that the original decision to manufacture a British atomic bomb had been taken by an inner caucus of Attlee's 1945 government, without Parliament's knowledge. There was the experience of seeing the Labour leadership refuse to accept the unilateralist vote at the 1960 conference, and the loss of the unilateralists' policy next year because of a fear of "rocking the boat". There was the hailing of "Aldermaston Marchers in the Cabinet" as *Sanity* headlined it after the 1964 election, to be followed by the disillusionment because nothing changed, or if it did, it was for the worse; for somehow those particular marchers managed to endorse the ordering of Polaris submarines and support for America in Vietnam.

There was the realisation of how powerful a hostile press could be. Not only was there almost total opposition amongst the national press to CND's aims, despite the substantial support indicated by opinion polls, but reporting of the movement was usually irresponsible, inaccurate and damaging. There was also the refusal of the BBC to televise *The War Game*, a film it had actually commissioned. And there was direct experience of the political bias of the judicial system. An instance was that of the six members of the Committee of 100 who appeared at the Old Bailey in February, 1962, charged under the Official Secrets Act with organising a demonstration at Wethersfield USAF base that was "prejudicial to the safety and interest of the state". They saw their attempt to produce expert witnesses who wished to testify that their action was actually protective of the state's safety, ruled inadmissable on the grounds that whatever is Crown policy is necessarily in the interests of the State.

Years of campaigning demonstrated that the political system did not view our demands as reforms of policy but as radical change that it refused to contemplate. The determination of governments to hold on to a military (and nuclear) world role, the links between industry and arms production and sales, and the links between the civil and military nuclear programmes have shown how closely wedded the possession of nuclear arms is to almost every other aspect of government policy. Perhaps the most devastating realisation has been that the Labour Party, at least when in power, has been as much wedded to such policies as the Conservative Party. Thus, there seemed to be no clear route to achieving nuclear disarmament. To many people, the anarchist view that power is about being powerful, and that being powerful means hanging onto the most powerful weapons, seemed broadly justified. Some people used this kind of analysis to take their concern with democracy, or with powerlessness as they saw it, into other fields, and to organise at the community level, trying to create forms of participation in basic issues such as housing, local amenities, education and industry.

What now? All sorts of conclusions can follow from what I have said so far, many of which would suggest the need for some radical restructuring of society. So do we have to achieve that kind of change before we see disarmament happening? We can't be sure. However nuclear war is too urgent an issue to delay acting on while we seek wider political change; further, we have the advantage over the earlier movement in that we can base our campaigning on the lessons it taught us.

We have to use our critical understanding of society and the way the political parties operate. I would argue that this has several implications. We will still be dependent on a political party in government to implement our demands, but I am sure that we must not trust any party merely to adopt our policies and then carry them through. The emphasis must be on building a mass, well-informed movement which commands such public support that any party claiming to be serious about "peace" will have to support it in order to be elected; and the movement must be sustained once that party has gained office. We must be prepared to publicise the limitations imposed on us by the political system. We must be careful about using petitions and encouraging letters to MPs and ministers. Such activities have a place; but we must recognise their limitations, and the danger of creating illusions about the extent to which Britain is a responsive democracy. There must be an emphasis on local activity to generate widespread, vocal support, with groups tackling nuclear issues in their localities. This may include sustaining and developing the nuclear free zone policies which many local authorities have adopted, and demands should be made that they act in accord with such stands, persuading them to refuse to co-operate with national government requirements about civil defence and military establishments.

Our critical understanding of the system will also endorse the legitimacy of non-violent civil disobedience. Whilst CND may not want to organise civil disobedience (because not everyone feels able to be involved in it and because of the special responsibilities it entails) I am convinced that there should be no question about CND's support for civil disobedience, appropriately used.

Finally, it is crucial that our campaigning is persuasive, and not alienating. This means thinking about the symbolism of our actions, particularly when they are dependent on the media for communication. We must be concerned not to make points or shout out our anger to satisfy ourselves but to get across to others the dangers that we all face, encouraging them to become involved in the Campaign. We need the respect of people who are at present indifferent or hostile to us. We need a movement of non-violence that epitomises the positive values of truth and concern that are so lacking in the system we criticise, and which commands overwhelming support rather than depending on one segment of the political arena.

CND and the Churches
Paul Oestreicher

Since the conversion of the Emperor Constantine to Christianity the major churches of Christendom have — broadly speaking — accepted war as a necessary evil in the world as it is. In many epochs Christians have sought to limit war, to civilise it. They have also often been instigators of it. "Christian" history is not characterised by peace. Christians cannot credibly claim that war is the product of a pagan world.

Yet the early Church was pacifist. So, on any reasonable reading of the New Testament, was Jesus. Non-pacifists generally accept that but say that Jesus had a special and unique vocation which is possibly also laid on a select few of his followers. Some Christians have never accepted such arguments. There has always been a Christian anti-war lobby: the so-called historic peace churches (among them the Quakers) and individuals in all other churches.

And then there are others who have taken the doctrine of the just (i.e. justifiable) war seriously. It is a medieval doctrine accepted by both the Catholic and Protestant traditions laying down stringent rules about what constitutes such a war and how it may be conducted. What is clear beyond all reasonable argument is that nuclear war could never fulfil the conditions of a just war.

No respectable theologian today still puts forward the Old Testament idea of the Holy War (i.e. the crusade). The choice that remains is between Christian pacifism and the doctrine of the just war. Nuclear war qualifies on neither count.

That only leaves the very abstruse moral argument about threatening nuclear war in order to avoid it — and intending not to implement the threat. That is obviously a barren debate, although it occupies a lot of people's time and energy and cannot therefore simply be dismissed.

What all this points to is the fact that increasingly CND should have the self-confidence to recognise that — in a secular context — it is actually putting forward a position that the churches, on the basis of their own faith and tradition, should be supporting. At every level CND should therefore be seeking such support.

Christians who, for their part, accept the moral and political case for unilateral nuclear disarmament should therefore both be active within CND – and its Christian sub-section – and active within their particular church to persuade others of their duty to work and pray for the implementation of CND's policies. Enormous psychological barriers remain to be overcome. Many Christians are simply afraid of anything political. Others are so afraid of communism that anything that even appears to be "wet" in this context is suspect. At this point careful and sustained prayer and argument are essential – and a great deal of tolerance. The centuries-old traditions of nationalism and social conservatism cannot be overcome in a decade or two.

It is important to realise that broadly speaking the leadership of the churches is more sympathetic than the grass roots. The Archbishop of Canterbury is typical of many. He has yet to be persuaded that unilateralism will not destabilise the precarious peace we have. But he also believes (and says) that loving our enemies is the only political policy the churches are authorised to pursue. "Perfect love", the scriptures say, "casts out fear" – and casting out fear is perhaps the churches' most important contribution to the whole debate.

Structurally, CND can and must relate to many Christian bodies which are more or less sympathetic. None of them is hostile. First there is the British Council of Churches which officially believes Britain should cease to be an independent nuclear power and which has thought constructively on the question for many years. There are the social responsibility departments of all the major denominations. Within them there is much sympathy: and many critical questions are asked. And there are the small but not unimportant Church peace organisations which in any case support CND policy. The best organised is the Roman Catholic Pax Christi organisation which exists both nationally and internationally, as does the fellowship of Reconciliation. And then there is the world-wide Christian network which is increasingly concerned with this issue. A group of American Catholic Bishops are one of several vanguards in this debate. Away out ahead is the Church of Holland. The witness of East German protestantism is perhaps even more significant in this context. Britain too, of course, has its individual prophets in this cause like Dr Kenneth Greet, of the Methodist Church. Nor is it mere chance that Canon Collins headed CND in its original phase, while today Msgr. Bruce Kent gives it inspired leadership.

In Britain and world-wide the followers of Jesus of Nazareth are being called to join this war against weapons which could destroy us all and are therefore a direct affront to the Creator. Yet the Christian place is a humble one and must – in the light of history – be a penitent one. On no major public occasion should CND's message be heard without its Christian component. On no major Christian occasion should the Church be allowed to forget that a failure to support the struggle against a nuclear holocaust would be a betrayal of the Gospel. That Christians, like others, will continue to disagree with each other is perhaps an inevitable fact in a fallen world. The need for both sides to listen sensitively to each other has never been greater. The need for passion and compassion in this spiritual struggle is almost self-evident. While all this continues, the need for the Church to help break down barriers of prejudice, pride and fear is a challenge central to its very existence. In a Church obedient to its Master, CND has a potential ally of inestimable worth.

Postscript

When the above was written, I did not dare hope that the publication of *The Church and the Bomb* by a working party reporting to the General Synod of the Church of England would have caused a major national stir. Chaired by the Bishop of Salisbury, that group of seven Christians came to practical conclusions which in many respects resemble CND policy. The Tory MP who thereupon called the Church of England "CND at prayer" was — from his own point of view — crying wolf. The Church of England has some way to go before it commits itself as an institution to the "unilateral steps within a multilateral process" which the Report recommends. By the time this book is published the General Synod will have debated the book. It will probably have commended it to Christians as an important contribution to a vital debate. It may have gone further and actually endorsed the recommendations in the book. Or it may have rejected them. The debate will without doubt have been followed with great interest by the public and with some trepidation by the Government.

Meanwhile the churches of the Reformed tradition in Germany have declared that to use or threaten to use nuclear weapons is not just immoral but incompatible with the Christian faith. And perhaps most important of all the American Catholic Bishops have written a letter to the faithful which radically calls in question the ethics of deterrence. Peace has moved rapidly from the margins to the centre of the churches' agenda. That is more than a step in the right direction.

CND and the Unions
Ruth Longoni and Walter Wolfgang

When the post-war consensus on foreign and defence policies broke down in the late fifties, trade union stalwarts saw their nephews and nieces — many trade unionists themselves — marching in the early Aldermaston marches and expressing a new critical awareness. Those who had long nurtured private and public doubts about establishment policies no longer felt isolated. Others were made aware of the problems of the nuclear age.

In 1959 the General and Municipal Workers' Union voted at its conference for unilateral nuclear disarmament. Although this commitment was later reversed, the breach had been made. Frank Cousins became the general secretary of the Transport and General Workers Union and gave notable support to the Campaign for Nuclear Disarmament. Trade-union votes secured both the TUC and the Labour Party for unilateral nuclear disarmament in 1960. Although this was reversed at key trade-union conferences and consequently at the TUC and Labour Party conference in 1961, a generation of trade union activists had become committed supporters of unilateral nuclear disarmament. The influence of these activists helped, in changed circumstances, to secure the adoption of unilateralist resolutions by the 1972 and 1973 Labour Party conferences. Nuclear disarmament was not however a dominant concern during the 1970s and many learned to live with the bomb.

The realisation throughout Europe in 1979 and 1980 that mutually assured destruction (MAD) had been abandoned and that nuclear war-fighting strategies provided the "justification" for planning to deploy Cruise missiles and Pershing II's created a new burst of awareness, which took root in Britain in 1980. There is much stronger support for unilateral nuclear disarmament than during the 1960s, resulting in the adoption of unilateralism by the Labour Party Conferences in 1980, 1981 and 1982 and by the TUC in 1981 and 1982 with unprecedented majorities.

At the time of writing twenty-one national unions and around 350 trade-union organisations are affiliated to National CND, and many more to their local CND group or region. Others, like the NUT, have a unilateralist policy but are not affiliated to CND.

Winning union policies for unilateralism is important. Union conference decisions are designed to be a culmination of discussion and winning ideas in the branches. They stimulate wider discussion, raise awareness of the issues involved, and provide a lever by which trade unions can be brought into active participation in the campaign.

Along with working for policy decisions must go activity to involve trade unionists in campaigning. Local contact by CND groups, regional or national officers, with their counterparts in the union structures, at a personal level, over a period of time, will help to establish the ways and means of translating resolutions into action.

Union branches, shop stewards' schools and district and regional committees should be asked to have a CND speaker at their meetings; permission should be sought for CND stalls and exhibitions at union meetings and conferences. Co-operation between CND and the unions needs to be a two-way process: CND groups should invite union representatives to address their branch meetings on topics relevant to campaigning in the trade-union movement.

CND members who are trade unionists need to play their part in defending unions from attempts to weaken them, such as those embodied in the Tebitt legislation which seeks to withdraw immunity from court action from trade unions and their members unless they can show that their dispute is "wholly or mainly" connected with terms and conditions of employment. The implications are clear for our strategy which seeks to build support for industrial and political action against nuclear weapons.

CND aims to build the Campaign at the workplace and there are a number of workplace groups established; these might be stimulated by leafleting of workplaces, but the impetus must come from within. In factories where military production is undertaken the setting up of such a group may lead to questioning in a constructive way the nature of the product and plans for alternative production.

Trade Union CND, which is a specialist section of CND, is developing policies in a number of areas. These include involving local government unions in the nuclear-free zones campaign, and developing the idea of an arms conversion bill to give legal backing to conversion schemes. It is in the context of arms conversion and challenging the arms economy that the slogan "Jobs not Bombs" is realistic. The damaging effect of arms expenditure on the economy and jobs is now widely realised. Countries which spend the most on arms have the worst economic prospects. Japan which spends 1 per cent of GNP on arms, compared with over 5 per cent by Britain, has been free to invest in other sectors of the economy and has a rate of 8 per cent growth in manufacturing productivity compared with 4 per cent in Britain.* Arms spending is inflationary; the industry is capital-intensive and employs fewer workers per pound than do other sectors of the economy. Weapons are paid for at the expense of essential public services. CND recognises, however, that the jobs of many workers depend on the nuclear arms industry and that arms conversion needs to be incorporated into its strategy for nuclear disarmament.

Many workers would prefer not to have their skills exploited in the manufacture of death machines. Some of the most detailed and advanced plans for alternative production have come from workers in this sector. In 1975, in response to redundancies, the Lucas Aerospace shop stewards combine committee drew up proposals for alternative products to the engine-management components they produced for both civil and military aviation. The Lucas workers argued that where competitive pressures and production for profit led to redundancies, the alternative should be based on meeting social needs. The workers' designs included a self-propelling "hobcart" for children suffering from spina bifida; a prototype heat pump, able to provide cheap heating; and portable kidney machines which would save the lives of those now denied the scarce NHS resources. The Corporate Plan presented by the stewards was realistic and workable. The company, however, refused to negotiate, and government ministers failed to back the workers.

* CND's pamphlet: *The Arms Drain: Job Risk and Industrial Decline* by Tim Webb.

The Centre for Alternative Industry and Technological Systems (CAITS), set up by the Lucas Aerospace shop stewards at the North East London Polytechnic makes available information on arms conversion. In 1978 CAITS worked with the TGWU to prepare a plan, based on alternative products, to ensure the job security of their members in dockyards and ordnance factories and depots. The TGWU has produced a policy document arguing for alternative work for their members in military establishments. After the Second World War, eight million workers were redeployed from military production in Britain within eighteen months. If the will is there it can be done.

CND can play a part in co-operating with unions in gathering information about the effects of arms production on the workers involved and on the economy, and in presenting the alternatives. Trade-union federations such as the Confederation of Shipbuilding and Engineering unions and the TUC at national and regional levels can be involved in this.

While we cannot wait for government action to start this process, the role of government is vital in making available the necessary resources. A government Office for Defence Conversion should be established to provide alternative work for those losing their jobs now, and in order that a future government, committed to nuclear disarmament and reduction of arms spending, can implement the transfer.

To bring about a government with such policies and ensure their implementation requires the most broadly based campaigning by the peace movement and its allies. The 11 million-strong trade-union movement represents a powerful component in an alliance for peace. Much good-will and commitment to CND exists among trade unionists. The task before us is to make this potential a reality.

CND and the Labour Party
David Griffiths

There have always been close links between CND's development and Labour Party politics. The Labour Left in particular has been a rich source of support for CND, and the main channel through which its case has been voiced in Parliament. At the same time unilateralism, has been one of the major issues distinguishing Left and Right within the Party.

But there have been significant changes over the years in the character of the relationship. CND's early rise and fall was crucially centred on developments inside the Party. The story has often enough been told of how unilateralism carried the day at Labour's 1960 Scarborough conference, only to be reversed the following year. What is interesting is that, in most accounts of CND's early days, these events feature as *the* climatic moments of the entire movement, while few would see the comparable unilaterialist victories at the

1980, 1981 and 1982 Party Conferences as the *central* feature of CND's spectacular rebirth over the last three years.

This is not to say that these victories have been unimportant for the Party. They have prompted many in the Centre genuinely to rethink their traditional position on defence, as the emergence of a 120-strong CND group in the Parliamentary Party shows; they have played their part in pushing some on Labour's Right towards the SDP; and they once drew a threat from Denis Healey, the Party's deputy leader and foreign affairs spokesman, not to serve in a future Labour Cabinet unless the policy is reversed.

But they are less significant for CND than the 1960/61 debacle, because CND's own approach has changed. The leaders of the "first wave" saw formally winning the Party to a unilateralist policy as a crucial strategic objective. Accordingly, 1960 seemed a more momentous victory than 1980; but 1961 was correspondingly a greater defeat than any shift in Labour policy could now be, and one factor among others in initiating CND's long slide from its early heights. Twenty years and four Labour governments later, there is a good deal more realism about the relationship between Labour Conference decisions and the performance of Labour governments — and accordingly less temptation to put all CND's eggs in the Labour basket.

But the comparison between 1960 and 1980 glosses over another telling episode. For unilateralism *also* carried the day at the Party's 1972 and 1973 Conferences — and nobody took much notice. Come 1980, indeed, these decisions had been forgotten by almost everybody, and the press and Party activists alike presented that year's decision as the first breakthrough (or disaster) since 1961. To my mind the moral of the story is clear — and crucial. The 1960 and 1980 decisions had major political repercussions because they reflected the strength of the popular movement for disarmament *outside* the Party. The 1972/73 decisions mattered far less because, though carefully nursed through the Party's constitutional machinery, they had no comparable strength behind them.

If we ask, then, how CND and the Labour Party should relate to each other, the answer must go something like this. A popular movement whose objectives require governmental action has to win the support of a major party capable of winning office. For CND the Labour Party is, for the present, the only serious candidate, and thus a vital area of work for the Campaign. But the way to "win" the Party, and hold it on course in Government, is not to become absorbed in the intricacies of its internal processes, still less to insist that CND must wed itself to socialist politics and enter any kind of formal relationship with the Party. Such approaches, by destroying the extraordinary coalition which CND represents, would fundamentally weaken the movement for British nuclear disarmament. In doing so they would, paradoxically, *reduce* the likelihood of a future Labour government implementing CND's policies — for if it does so the pressure of mass opinion will have been more influential than exactly which conferences resolutions were carried by what majorities.

The proper relationship thus mixes a degree of fraternity with respect for CND's autonomy. The renaissance of the past two years has taught us something about how this kind of relationship can work out in practical terms. The Labour Party caught the rebirth of mass concern about nuclear weapons at quite an early stage, and its 20,000-strong demonstration against Trident, Cruise and higher arms spending, in June 1980, played an important part in building the momentum towards CND's much larger demonstration four months later. With a mass movement well and truly re-established, the Labour Party has wisely refrained from taking an independent lead again, but has given formal and practical support nationally to subsequent initiatives from CND, END and the World Disarmament Campaign; and it has continued to produce its own campaigning material.

At local level, meanwhile, Labour Party members have played a substantial role alongside others in initiating CND activity. An important and distinctive contribution has been the backing for the Campaign from Labour local authorities. They have assisted the movement's propaganda by declaring themselves nuclear-free zones, pointed to the futility of the civil defence preparations for which they are required to take responsibility, and given material support to local CND groups.

Beyond this kind of mutual support, there are at least two other areas of fruitful interaction for CND and the Labour Party. First, Labour can learn much from CND — as from other recent movements such as the Anti-Nazi League — about political styles and strategies. For too long Labour, Left and Right alike, has been wedded to an almost entirely electoral politics: bouts of electioneering proper alternate with rather introverted party meetings where resolutions are adopted making demands on the duly elected representatives. Missing from this, but central to CND's politics, has been any concept of reaching out in imaginative and involving ways to win active support for the Party's policies — the only successful guarantee of their eventual implementation.

In the policy field, in contrast, Labour can potentially do something which CND, because of the breadth of support which is also its strength, will always find difficult. It can formulate a positive non-nuclear defence policy for Britain, taking us beyond the vital (but in itself negative) starting point of unilateralism. In the time remaining before the next general election this could, indeed, be Labour's most important contribution.

CND and the Nationalist Parties
Isobel Lindsay

The Welsh and Scottish nationalist parties have a long record of opposition to nuclear weapons which has its origins in the underlying philosophical position of these two parties. There are three principal strands in the outlook of Plaid and the SNP which have made them hostile to any nuclear military role.

In the first place, the British imperial tradition has been an important factor in the development and maintenance of a nuclear-based defence policy. The arguments used by successive governments have revolved around such ideas as "seats at the top table", maintaining Britain's international role, being able to stand up on our own to the Russians. There has been an implicit belief in Britain as a Great Power, playing a key role in international decision-making.

Virtually by definition, Plaid and the SNP have been hostile to the "Great Britain" concept and the imperial tradition. They require the recognition and acceptance of the role of Wales, Scotland, England and Ireland as small to medium nations without a big-power military role. This change in perception would remove not all, but an important part of the case for nuclear weapons. It would also greatly reduce the financial capacity to pursue an independent nuclear system.

Second, the Welsh and Scottish nationalists have been naturally sympathetic to decentralised political structures, small-scale development and environmental protection. These represent political attitudes fundamentally hostile to the nuclear state, which demands a high degree of centralisation in order to make the system feasible and is prepared to risk grave environmental damage in order to further its defence objectives. Third, Scotland and Wales are both countries with a strong radical tradition — on the whole hostile to Conservative thinking. It is natural that their nationalist parties should reflect this and that their general political orientation is to the left rather than the right. This is true in defence as in other issues.

Scotland, in addition, has particularly strong reasons for adopting an anti-nuclear stance since she has a very high concentration of nuclear or nuclear-related installations. These comprise not only the well-known bases like Holy Loch and Faslane but nuclear weapon stores at Glen Douglas, maintenance and servicing of submarines at Rosyth, important surveillance facilities in the north, and a profusion of other certain targets in the event of war. The proposed Trident development has served as a reminder that many of these potential targets are situated close to the most densely-populated area in Scotland.

The SNP has opposed nuclear developments at least since the introduction of the Holy Loch base. In 1968 its opposition to nuclear bases was combined with opposition to NATO membership. This position was changed in the mid 1970s to support for non-nuclear NATO membership i.e. the Norwegian option, and reverted again in 1981 to opposition to membership of any military alliance based on nuclear strategy. The anti-nuclear position has included opposition to the nuclear power programme and proposed dumping of nuclear waste. Any time the question of nuclear bases has been put to a vote, they have always been opposed by an overwhelming majority.

The record of Plaid Cymru has been even longer and more impressive. They first opposed nuclear military developments immediately after Hiroshima and Nagasaki, and they have continued consistently to support this position with no internal opposition. They have also always opposed NATO membership. Nuclear power has been a more recent debate within Plaid and they have opposed this.

There are some who see nationalism per se as hostile to the interests of international peace. This attitude arises from a failure to distinguish between nationalism and imperialism or racialism. The need for community, and for a distinctive collective as well as individual identity, is very basic to the highly social animals we are.

Most of us in CND recognise that the problems of weapons of mass destruction are with mankind permanently. If we are successful in achieving disarmament, we cannot escape the fact that the knowledge will remain, and that our problem in the long run is one of changing attitudes and structures to avoid any recurrence of the arms race. One of the factors which we will have to concern ourselves with is the inherent temptation for the large, powerful state to pursue an imperial role. Without the interference of the large states, the disputes of the small ones could remain local and containable. The very large states also make it difficult to run genuine international organisations because of their disproportionate power. Our concern for peace must lead us to explore the structural factors which in the long run will help to maintain it. In this context the small nation movements have something to say.

CND in Scotland and Wales is fortunate in having the unqualified support of both the Labour and Nationalist Parties. The parties can distribute CND information through their communications networks; they can help local CND groups to get established; and they can offer experience in political campaigning which many non-party CND activists may lack. What could damage the Campaign would be to become over-identified with any *one* political group: it must be as even-handed as possible in its co-operation with different political parties.

Finally, a word of caution; political party activists all run the risk of becoming stale and cynical about campaigning techniques. They often remain stuck in the grooves of what was effective five years ago, or even twenty years ago. The "educational" emphasis of the revived CND has surprised a number of experienced politicians by its popularity. By all means use the skills, resources and experience of political parties; but also let CND carve out its own forms of political communication.

CND and the Liberal-SDP Alliance
Robert Fyson

There have always been Liberals active in CND. This is scarcely surprising, since the Liberal Party's long history includes a radical tradition of anti-war protest, exemplified in the Liberal onslaught on the "methods of barbarism" used in the Boer War, and the opposition of many Liberals, then including Bertrand Russell, to the First World War.

At the time when CND began, the Liberal Party adopted a policy of opposition to Britain's possession of her *own* nuclear weapons, which has been maintained ever since. The 1958 Liberal Party Assembly voted by a huge majority for an end to British H-bomb tests and renunciation of the "independent deterrent", which went beyond official Labour policy at that time. And some Liberals went further and became staunch supporters of CND. But, at a time when the two-party alternation of majority Tory and Labour governments still seemed to be an unalterable law of British politics, the Liberals were not taken very seriously by most people; and the political strategy of the CND leadership was firmly oriented towards the return of a Labour government which might, it was hoped, at least go part of the way towards implementing CND policies.

These hopes were disappointed by the Labour governments of the 1960s and 1970s. And, partly as a result of this disappointment, the Liberal Party became more radical. The Young Liberals, especially, campaigned vigorously against the arms trade and against British support for the Americans in the Vietnam war. When, in the late 1970s, nuclear power as an energy source became a controversial issue, the Liberal Party became the only major political party to oppose nuclear energy.

The revival of CND found the Liberal Party larger, more radical, and getting more public attention than it had when CND was first launched. At the party Assembly in September 1980, about one-third of the delegates voted for complete unilateral nuclear disarmament, but a resolution supporting NATO orthodoxy was narrowly passed. A year later, however, in September 1981 the Assembly agreed by 752 votes to 485 to a motion which declared that "the escalation and spread of nuclear weapons is the major threat to world peace" and that "Britain should take the initiative in calling for a European nuclear-free zone and opposing the deployment of Cruise missiles in Europe" and committing the Liberal Party "as a first step, to reject and campaign against the siting of Cruise missiles in Britain". This is now, therefore, official Liberal Party policy. And in November 1982 The Party Council voted to support non-violent direct action against Cruise and a freeze on the manufacture and deployment of nuclear weapons.

So far, so good. But the same Assembly saw the acceptance, by an overwhelming majority, of the formation of an Alliance between the Liberals and the new Social Democratic Party to contest the next General Election as equal partners. The founders of the SDP are, of course, former Labour ministers, and one of the issues which has led them to leave the Labour Party is their opposition to unilateral nuclear disarmament: the "Gang of Four" and the other MPs who have joined the SDP are opposed to CND and its policies. It is hard to say much more about SDP defence policy at this early stage. But not all SDP members agree with the MPs — for instance, an opinion survey in November 1981 showed that 22 per cent of SDP members believed in unilateral nuclear disarmament, which isn't bad for a start. Despite the views of the leadership, the absence of a fixed political tradition within the SDP could make it more amenable than the older parties to new ideas for alternative, non-nuclear, defence policies.

It would be foolish to minimise the difficulties which stand in the way of the Alliance adopting, or, if it forms a government, implementing a policy of nuclear disarmament. The Liberals' anti-Cruise Assembly decision was a major victory, and a significant break with the party's previous adherence to NATO orthodoxy; but David Steel, anxious not to upset the Gang of Four, publicly opposed the new policy immediately after the Assembly vote. Only three of the present twelve Liberal MPs (David Alton, Bill Pitt and Richard Wainwright) support the Party's anti-Cruise policy, and the Parliamentary defence spokesman, Lord Mayhew, is a veteran opponent of CND. Serious struggles over defence policy may lie ahead.

But there are real signs of hope in the large numbers of Liberal and SDP activists who now see nuclear disarmament as their political priority. Each party now has its own CND and Peace Group. Prominent Liberals, including Viv Bingham, Party President 1981-2, and many prospective parliamentary candidates, have given CND their support; Liberal councillors have been in the forefront of those pressing for local authority "nuclear-free zones" and questioning the value of civil defence expenditure; Liberal commitment to Europe has led many Liberals to support the movement for European Nuclear Disarmament.

I am not suggesting that CND supporters must necessarily join the Liberals or the SDP. Obviously, there is very important work to be done for CND in the Labour Party, the focus of most past CND pressure, in other parties and outside party politics altogether. It would flout the spirit of a broadly based popular movement to associate it exclusively with any one political party — or even two! But, especially at a time of political volatility and uncertainty such as the present, it would be very foolish if CND were to neglect the Alliance parties: they could well come to hold the balance of power in Parliament, or even form a government. All that those of us in the Liberal/SDP Alliance are asking is that the movement should recognise the importance of our work for peace and disarmament within the Alliance. More information can be obtained from CND, 11 Goodwin St, London N4: we invite the active and urgent support of those who share our position.

CHAPTER EIGHT
Direct action – past, present and future

In CND's early years, the idea of direct action against nuclear weapons, and in particular the tactic of civil disobedience, prompted a good deal of disagreement within the movement. In this chapter **Pat Arrowsmith** traces the changing pattern of attitudes to direct action within the movement from the early years to the present. **Bruce Kent** discusses the choice facing each individual and the consequences; and **Tony Simpson** describes the success of a campaign in Wales where non-violent civil disobedience was an important part of the activity.

The Direct-Action Debate
Pat Arrowsmith

What is non-violent direct action? – books have been written about this. Most people would probably agree that it includes the range of activities carried out in Gandhi's and Luther King's campaigns: obstruction, occupations, boycotts, tax refusal, industrial action, illegal leafleting ... But it is not an easy term to define and there was considerable debate in the disarmament movement twenty years ago about what it meant. CND did not, for instance, seem to equate direct action with industrial action: at annual conferences there was always a separate debate prompted by separate resolutions on the two types of action. There still is.

When CND started in early 1958 the idea of a mere march from London to Aldermaston was unheard of. As organiser, I had quite a job persuading the eminently respectable, self-appointed CND Executive Committee even to sponsor it. As for obstructing work on rocket bases – that would be outrageous. Many and prolonged were the wrangles about direct action by nuclear disarmers twenty years ago. Breaking democratically passed laws was undemocratic argued the constitutionalists. No it wasn't, the direct actionists countered – not when something so utterly undemocratic as planned genocide was involved. Moreover the government had decided to make the bomb without consulting the electorate – surely that was undemocratic? But what about CND's image, pursued the constitutionalists – we wouldn't impress people if we did extraordinary illegal things like sit-downs in front of lorries; we wouldn't gain support and win over the working class that way ... As for industrial action against the bomb, that was both far too radical and a pipe-dream ... And so the argument continued at conference after conference, on television programme after television programme ... Direct action was taken anyway – obstructions, small strikes ...

And direct actionists argued among themselves about the matter. There was divided opinion in the Direct Action Committee Against Nuclear War (DAC) about the ethics of blocking lorries: did this constitute violence towards the drivers? If the drivers responded violently towards the demonstrators were the latter not themselves being violent by provoking such a response? And what about damaging property? Would using wire-cutters to get through a security fence amount to violent sabotage? Did non-violence entail absolute openness or could initial plans be made discreetly, illegal leaflets be distributed secretly? ... It was (perhaps still is) as hard to achieve an agreed definition of non-violence as of direct action.

Then, when the Committee of 100 was launched (many of its members being also grass roots CND members just as the DAC's supporters were) the question arose: were direct action and civil disobedience the same thing? If not, were they of equal value? This prompted debate about the usefulness of publicity for its own sake as distinct from the intrinsic value of an action — witholding tax, obstructing nuclear bases etc. The early Committee of 100 demonstrations were large sit-downs in public places (Whitehall and Trafalgar Square) which in themselves had no direct connection with missile sites and bomb plants – unlike the earlier DAC projects, which were attempts to stop work on and occupy bases. The Committee of 100 demonstrations were conceived of as civil disobedience which would fill the nation's jails. Actual direct action might or might not result in imprisonment (it didn't always). Certain Committee of 100 members argued that it was pointless, even possibly counterproductive, to block innocuous streets; the action should be at the bases. Others (at first the majority) said that to get thousands breaking the law conspicuously in city centres would achieve more publicity, hence be more useful, than getting (inevitably) fewer people to take action at remote bases. Eventually the Committee did move out from city streets to the airfields. Later, when the Vietnam war was in full swing, the debate changed to violence versus non-violence – it was the Grosvenor Square punch-up era. Amazingly, CND, after years of agonising debate about direct action, passed a resolution committing the Campaign almost by mistake to supporting this kind of action. The Vietnam Solidarity Campaign was planning a potentially enormous and (many feared) violent march on the US Embassy. A small DAC descendant, the November Non-Violent Action Committee, decided to inject some *satyagraha** into the anti-Vietnam war campaign by organising a non-violent "siege" of the head office of a firm supplying equipment for US bombers. When the CND annual conference voted in favour of supporting this project because it was non-violent no one – not even Peggy Duff –

* satyagraha: the Gandhian term for non-violent resistance.

immediately realised what had happened.

Since the days of the DAC and Committee of 100 (perhaps because of these groups) direct action has become relatively acceptable, even normal. Motorways have been blocked, factories occupied, animals liberated, nuclear power station construction impeded ... Today the great divide between constitutionalists and direct actionists no longer exists. This may be partly because the state is becoming more repressive. Admittedly, twenty years ago *THEY* could always, when the felt like it, find a law for you to have broken − for instance the 1361 Justices of the Peace Act, which in 1959 put the entire DAC in preventive detention for two months for refusing to promise not to continue organising the action it was busy planning. But nowadays, with more legal restrictions on picketing, occupations and strikes; a greater tendency to ban simple marches; greater use of such laws as the Incitement to Disaffection Act to reduce freedom of expression, it may be even easier than it was twenty years ago for the authorities to arrest people for doing things that were never envisaged as direct action or civil disobedience. The disctinction between lawful and unlawful activity is thus less clear than it used to be. Anyone who had chosen to defy the ban (had it not been lifted) by marching from the Faslane Polaris base in 1981 would have found they had committed civil disobedience ...

Today, unlike twenty years ago, CND is committed to direct (including industrial) action; it is not split on the issue. Up and down the country discussions and workshops on direct action are being held and nuclear disarmers are starting to take direct action again. The debate now is not about *whether* to organise it but *how*.

Direct Action and CND in the 1980s − a personal view
Bruce Kent

My claims to write a section on the theme of direct action are fairly thin. What I have to say comes from an observer rather than a practitioner − at least so far. Recently I met Philip Berrigan on a visit to Britain and Germany, and in front of people like him, and the many others in America and elsewhere, who have suffered long terms of inprisonment as witnesses against the nuclear evil, the only proper attitude is respect.

It is perfectly true that the divisions, hard and fast, that existed for many in the Sixties, between those for and those against direct action, now seem largely to have disappeared. At its 1981 conference CND, as a movement, not only agreed to support "considered non-violent direct actions" but went on to say that it would "be willing to organize and lead national direct action if the occasion arose". This decision was confirmed by our 1982 conference, and the occasion is looming up fairly rapidly on the horizon just now, as the date for the deployment of Cruise missiles comes closer. Nor should this be a surprise. Even for conformist consciences there must be a point beyond which secular law ceases to bind. It was for instance actually a Lord Chancellor of England, Thomas More, who died on the scaffold for breaking the civil law, declaring that he died "the King's good Servant, but God's first".

The choice for each individual – and conference resolutions do not by-pass such choices – is to decide when positive law should be disobeyed, what form such disobedience should take, and what effect if any is being sought. Sometimes there can be no possible question of effect. Franz Jagerstatter died alone and unknown in his Berlin prison in 1943, executed as a conscientious objector, not because he thought his death would influence anyone else, but simply because it was intolerable to him to have to take the unconditional military oath.

I suspect, however, that most of the direct action which is discussed today has in it not only the prophetic element, but also the hope that it will turn out to be an effective instrument of campaigning: that it will stop something happening or it will wake up and involve in the struggle those not yet active.

At this point Saul Alinsky's *Rules for Radicals* becomes very important. It is clear enough that some direct action gets off the ground for the wrong reasons and actually turns out to be quite counter-productive. Direct action cannot be a short-cut means of avoiding the hard, boring and routine work of mass campaigning and public education, of leafleting and street theatre, of petitioning and film shows, of debates and school visits. Alinsky was very keen on the idea that any activist who wants to be effective has got to start from where people are and go with them; never to start from a position so far ahead that people do not identify but simply get turned off. Direct action is not a thinly covered martyr complex or a moral short cut but part of a whole thought-out process. Hence the carefully chosen "considered" of the CND resolution which must involve joint planning and consultation in advance.

Equally well chosen was the phrase "non-violent". CND is not a pacifist organisation, so I speak personally when I say that I do not see how one can effect a qualitative change in a society by using the methods of violence of that society itself. "Let no man drag you down so low that you begin to hate him," said Martin Luther King, and real non-violence is no easy task when we are faced with the rich who crush the poor, the powerful who abuse the weak, or the many more who know exactly what is going on but keep their eyes shut. But, whether from an ideal or from a practical starting point, direct action which involves violence seems to me to be quite counter-productive and simply invites the forces of repression to do their worst. And they usually do. The power of the peace camps, which have spread so rapidly in recent months starting with Greenham Common, has been exactly that their aim was and is to be camps of peace.

I have, however, had to rethink some of my more conventional ideas about violence to property since the visit of Philip Berrigan. His latest "crime" was, with others, to destroy the nose cone of a nuclear missile with a hammer. Violence? Not in his eyes: simply a method of returning to nature what had already been perverted and made violent. I'm sure, in terms of conscience, he is quite right, as are those who use violence against the laboratory instruments of animal torture and sometimes go to prison for their pains. Nevertheless, any direct action which includes in its planning violence to property should surely be very well "considered". There may be a justification which comes from the highest motivation, but such actions may equally turn off very many who might otherwise have started to take a few steps in the right direction.

There is a last and sober thought for those of us now in CND and similar campaigns. Sometimes, I suspect, from the security of never having had to live in prison, that we have rather airy ideas about the consequences that may follow direct illegal action. Prisons are degrading places, and the run up to prison can be full of strain, uncertainty and humiliation. In my pocket I carry all the time a photo of Helen Allegranza who, as a staff member of the Committee of 100, was given a twelve-month prison sentence to be served in Holloway. Not long after her release, clearly still suffering from the shock effect of prison life, she committed suicide. I mention this not only as a mark of respect for her courage, but also as a reminder that direct action which is really considered will have taken into account the strengths of those involved, and the support groups they and their families are going to need. If we are talking about direct action on a large scale in the near future then there is a lot to be thought about and planned for now.

Finally, it is so important that we all respect each other's different speeds and different perceptions. In theory there should be now none of the splits of the 1960s. In practice it would be all too easy for people to get competitive about who is more involved and willing to suffer. There is a wide range of activities which will always have to go on in the peace movement — and those who decide that illegal action is not for them are not some inferior breed. The boring work of organisation, communication and even committees has a heroism of its own!

Direct Action at Bridgend — 1982
Tony Simpson

A campaign of direct action in Mid-Glamorgan has stopped work on a county nuclear bunker. Mid-Glamorgan CND occupied the site at Bridgend and set up a peace camp and picket on 24 January, only hours before the contractors, Fairclough Building, began work on a £400,000 contract to upgrade the County Wartime Headquarters in line with Home Office recommendations. CND warned councillors that this was in direct violation of Mid-Glamorgan's declaration of a Nuclear Free Zone on 17 December 1981. Though many councillors agreed, or were uneasy about the contract, they were told by County Clerk Hugh Thomas that they were under a statutory duty to provide civil defence facilities and that any alteration in the work could be viewed as a serious breach of contract. The chairman of the Public Protection Committee, who supported the work, persisted in calling the proposed building a "civil emergency centre" throughout discussions in council and with CND.

From the beginning of the occupation at the bunker site the Peace Camp was run by a consortium of eight CND groups from Mid-Glamorgan, and involved a picket of about 600 people. A campaign was launched with the slogan "Keep Mid-Glamorgan Nuclear Free" which was used on banners, posters and special badges. Some 50,000 copies of a campaign leaflet showing pictures of the bunkers, (there was already in existence a Central Government Nuclear Bunker for Wales, near Bridgend) were distributed in the valleys and towns of Mid-Glamorgan. A series of weekly public meetings on the site of the work brought in hundreds of people from the surrounding community and peace and labour groups, many of whom sent resolutions of protest to the County. The campaign therefore operated at a number of levels – on site, in the community, through the media and political channels. The local MP, Ray Powell, was lobbied and expressed serious concern about the project, raising questions in Parliament. CND lobbied every councillor and every council meeting. Each elected member was sent an information pack which included a research document showing the likely effects of nuclear weapons and full details of the local home defence network.*

After a Public Protection Committee meeting with us at the site of the work, a number of councillors began to express concern about the implications of the bunker project; four of them spoke at the weekly public meetings. On 18 February a delegation from CND was invited to address the council, after which the controlling (Labour) group issued a Statement of Intent, pledging themselves to pull out of civil defence and disassociate the bunker from nuclear war plans. But building work continued, and CND obtained plans showing details of blast-proof walls decontamination showers, air-filtration plants, and accommodation for over a hundred wartime officials for fourteen days. A report by Professor Alan Lipman, of the School of Architecture, University of Wales, proved beyond doubt that the reinforced steel and concrete base, and shuttering for sixteen-inch thick concrete walls,

* This illustrated booklet, H-Bomb on Ogur – a study of a Nuclear Attack in Wales, is now available from CND, 11 Goodwin Street, London N4 (75p including post and packing).

A full account of this action, entitled No Bunkers Here— has been jointly published by Mid-Glamorgan CND and Peace News and is available from CND national office, price £1.00.

showed the bunker was intended to resist detonations from nuclear weapons. This report was published on 8 March 1982, after six weeks of continuous occupation by the Peace Camp, and on the very day the contractors were preparing to construct the windowless blast walls. As concrete mixers arrived on the site, twenty protesters climbed to the top of the massive shuttering, using their bodies to prevent the pouring of the concrete into the cavities. A dangerous situation developed as workmen tried to force bodies out of the way, and finally concrete was poured over the demonstrators by the pumping machine. Other demonstrators tried to form a picket line to prevent the arrival of concrete mixers on the site but were frustrated by the police who persisted in calling the heavy lorries through the lines despite the dangers involved. The protest went on throughout the day; it involved equal numbers of men and women, some of whom put themselves at considerable risk in the cold, wet and muddy conditions. Tea and soup were passed up by supporters; the whole event was witnessed by senior police officers, TV cameras and press.

Elizabeth Goffe, who had been perched on the shuttering with us for most of the day, saw the television coverage later and recalls it:

> It did seem to me that the pictures of this protest on the TV screens that evening really had some effect. The completely non-violent nature of the action, which had only been taken when all the other usual means of democratic protest had been tried, had clearly made some impression on the viewers; and the serious determination of a pretty mixed bunch of men and women had brought home to people the seriousness, and urgency, felt by those taking part. This more dramatic phase of the campaign was only undertaken to urge the councillors who had promised to stop work on the bunker to show they meant what they said, as indeed we did.

The following day the Peace Camp demanded an emergency meeting of the full council to call off the work. The council admitted they had been inundated with letters, telephone calls and a concerted campaign involving visits and overnight telegrams at councillors' homes. At an emergency meeting on 15 March they agreed to halt work pending reports, and to support a resolution pledging "withdrawal from the Government's War Emergency Scheme", despite a stern warning from the Clerk that legal action, including surcharges, could follow. Within days a delegation from the council held a confidential meeting with the Home Office, where they were reminded of their statutory obligations to provide a civil defence team. Despite this, a meeting of the Public Protection Committee on 24 March, 1982, the same committee which had recommended the project, now agreed to cancel the contract and return the site to the Welsh Development Agency, who build factories not bunkers.

Mid-Glamorgan Peace Camp ended after fifty-seven days of siege. Daffodils (the flower of Wales and the symbol of the Wales Anti-Nuclear Alliance) were planted in a peace garden on the soil of the bunker. Peace graffiti appeared on the one remaining concrete wall, which showed cottage-style windows complete with potted plants, cats and lace curtains. The Peace Caravan, which was home for the protesters, has toured the valleys of South Wales, with a travelling exhibition illustrating the lessons of the campaign and showing pictures of the bunkers. Our plan is to make it available for other Peace Camps in Wales, to help continue the fight for peace in what is now the world's first country to be a declared Nuclear Free Zone.

Mid-Glamorgan CND say they and the public have learned a great deal from the Peace Camp. The most important lessons are that peace and democracy are indivisible, and that peace can only be achieved by non-violent means, through actions which try to make direct connections which people can understand. We found that people needed to help to actually see the implications of the bunker in terms of war plans, and then to see what could be done by ordinary citizens acting together. The bunker site stands as a monument to cold war folly. It has cost over £100,000, which could have been used for the county's public services (Mid-Glamorgan is the poorest country in Wales, with unemployment in some areas well over 20 per cent). People have begun to understand that it represents the whole philosophy behind nuclear war, especially the terrible waste of resources and erosion of liberties. The challenge for us in Mid-Glamorgan now is to construct a positive policy for peace from the ruins of the bunker, and the lessons it has taught us.

Postscript: December 1982

What of the Future?
Alasdair Beal

In the mid 1970s CND may have worked mainly as a pressure group: it is now a mass movement again. The change from pressure group to mass protest movement brings profound changes in the way the thing works. There is still an organisation to run and there are activities and campaigns to plan but somehow these cease to be predictable – either in their scale or their effect. Instead of resembling a motor car, which responds to accelerator and brake and must be paced with care to make the most of its (limited) supplies of fuel, it becomes more like a bonfire – the more fuel is thrown on, the higher leap the flames, throwing out sparks to start new fires and spread the conflagration. Predictable planning gives way to a dynamic process where one activity can stimulate another and their effects can become cumulative. Outside events, over which the Campaign has no control, can feed its development, sparking off new initiatives and charging planned events with wholly unplanned significance.

Thus CND's 80,000-strong demonstration in October 1980 had exceeded all expectations – when it was originally planned, 10,000 seemed an ambitious target. However, as was outlined in the Introduction, leaks of nuclear war plans, international crises and real accidental nuclear alerts combined to give anti-Cruise campaigns here and in Europe a massive boost. Suddenly, there was a nation-wide grassroots movement and it needed a national focus; instead of simply showing that the Campaign for Nuclear Disarmament existed, October 1980 revealed it as a considerable power in the land.

A year later, a quarter of a million marched in London and demonstrations in the capitals of Europe matched and exceeded this figure. European Nuclear Disarmament haunted NATO's nuclear planners.

In 1982, outside events have taken a hand once more. CND's national demonstration in June coincided not only with President Reagan's visit to Europe but also with a war in the South Atlantic which aroused strong emotions. The Government clearly hoped the "Falklands Factor" might break the formidable momentum of the anti-nuclear movement – if not in Europe, then at least in Britain. For a time, it seemed as if it might.

However, Autumn brought defeat for the Government's "Operation Hard Rock" civil defence exercise at the hands of an alliance of 'nuclear-free-zone' local councils, CND and scientists, whose "Operation Hard Luck" thoroughly discredited official notions that we can plan to survive a nuclear war. Autumn also brought an overwhelming victory for CND supporters at Labour Party Conference – and a string of defensive speeches from Government ministers, apprehensive that nuclear disarmament was looking increasingly like an election vote-winner. Opinion polls certainly back the impression that the idea of nuclear weapons as a means of defence is losing credibility among the public at large (even among Conservative voters, only 50 per cent support the Cruise and Trident missile programmes).

With the prospect of Cruise missiles in 1983 and a background like this, CND's 1982 Annual Conference, held in Sheffield, was clearly destined to be significant; but outside events once more conspired to give it a special sense of urgency. In Moscow, Brezhnev was dead; in Washington, there was a fuss over the new MX nuclear missile programme; and at Greenham Common, the Women's Peace Camp was broken up and protesters gaoled. Conference presented a unique opportunity to assess the state of the Campaign and to get some idea of its plans as it entered a critical year.

For a single issue campaign like CND, there is limited scope for the policy-making which is the staple diet of political conferences. Also "takeovers", "hijacks" and suchlike power struggles are much more difficult to wage in a Campaign composed of hundreds of independent-minded local groups. To a seasoned political journalist, accustomed to analysing feuds and splits, battles over policy or for power, it must have been rather confusing. What, for example, do you make of people whose badges proclaim that they are, variously, cat lovers, ageing hippies and well-meaning Guardian readers against the bomb?

On this showing, they are a diverse and determined bunch. In such a mass movement, politics is not a matter for abstract debate: the main objective is agreed, and debates are over tactics or differences of emphasis, rather than fundamental policy splits. Thus the subject of NATO produced a heated debate – not over whether or not CND should oppose Britain's membership (CND has agreed since 1960 that Britain cannot reasonably renounce its nuclear weapons yet remain under the NATO 'umbrella') but on the emphasis and timing of this demand. Activity in one area proceeds in parallel with activity in others – thus Conference supported *both* Non-Violent Direct Action and door-to-door canvassing; delegates who called for a special effort in the Labour and Trade Union movement also gave a rousing reception to a delegate from Tories Against Cruise and Trident. Through CND, diverse and local campaigns against Cruise and Trident have been able to link up. If people are obstinate enough to dedicate their efforts to stopping the nuclear arms race, they are hardly likely to have foisted on them policies they disagree with – they know that when time is short and the danger is great, co-operation is important, but blind obedience is a luxury they can ill afford. On the evidence of Sheffield,

November 1982, CND has strength, resilience and determination; its campaigners have the wit to see their differences and diversity as an asset rather than a liability.

Will direct action bring results to match the fine resolutions passed? Will CND's intervention in the General Election prove decisive? Will the hard slog of door-to-door canvassing bring a fundamental public shift?

It is hard to say, yet already since that Conference the pot has been stirred – in the USA the MX programme is meeting stiff opposition and the women's blockage of Greenham Common on December 13th may well herald more concerted direct action in the future.

On its 25th birthday, CND has a strength which probably surpasses *any* time in its history. It has a genuine chance, perhaps the last, of stopping the British end of the nuclear arms race and stimulating European nuclear disarmament. Whether it wins or loses no longer depends on the efforts of a handful of dedicated campaigners: CND has become a mass movement and its future depends on us all.

APPENDIX ONE

CND Chair and General Secretary, 1958-1982

CHAIR
Canon John Collins (1958-64)
Olive Gibbs (1964-67)
Sheila Oakes (1967-68)
Malcolm Caldwell (1968-70)
April Carter (1970-71)
John Cox (1971-77)
Bruce Kent (1977-79)
Hugh Jenkins (1979-81)
Joan Ruddock (1981-)

GENERAL SECRETARY
Peggy Duff (1958-67)
Dick Nettleton (1967-73)
Dan Smith (1974-75)
Duncan Rees (1976-79)
Bruce Kent (1979-)

APPENDIX TWO

CND Since 1970 – some figures

NATIONAL MEMBERS			Employees	CND Groups	Affiliated Organisations
Year	Total	Intake of New Members			
1970	2120	n.a.	5	50	n.a.
1971	2047	n.a.	4	n.a.	n.a.
1972	2389	105	4	n.a.	68
1973	2367	141	4	n.a.	140
1974	2350	217	4	n.a.	n.a.
1975	2536	225	3	60	158
1976	3220	440	3	n.a.	193
1977	2618	569	3	n.a.	236
1978	3220	602	3	102	293
1979	4287	559	4	150	274
1980	9000*	5000*	5	300	n.a.
1981	20000*	15000*	11	700*	n.a.
1982	50000*	30000*	25	1000*	1000*

Notes

n.a. – figures not available

* – approximate figures

Intake of new members does not necessarily equal exact difference between one year's total and the next, because of other factors – i.e. renewals, lapses etc of membership.

(Information supplied by Duncan Rees).

APPENDIX THREE

Films and Books on CND

Films

March to Aldermaston (35 minutes)
Lindsay Anderson film of first Aldermaston March　　　　1958

Rocket Site Story (20 minutes)
The only film record of the DAC demonstration at Swaffham in
December, 1958.　　　　1959

Aldermaston 1959 (10 minutes)
Brief record of second Aldermaston March.　　　　1959

Direct Action at Harrington (6 minutes)
Newsreel record of DAC demonstration at a Thor missile base in　　　1960
January, '60.

Deadly the Harvest (18 minutes)
Quaker film of third Aldermaston March.　　　　1960

The Walk (20 minutes)
Hilary Harris' film of '60-'61 11-month San Francisco-Moscow
walk against nuclear weapons.　　　　1962

Everyman I (20 minutes)
Story of the yacht built for direct action campaigns against nuclear
tests.　　　　1962

The Peacemakers (40 minutes)
John Freeman/Allan King, 1960's report on British and American
peace movement for Canadian TV.

All Against the Bomb (30 minutes)
CND's film made for the "Open Door" BBC series.　　　　1976

Poets Against the Bomb (30 minutes)
Film of CND benefit poetry reading in Chelsea Town Hall.　　　1981

Together We Can Stop the Bomb (20 minutes)
Film of 24 October '81 biggest CND demonstration to date.　　　1981

NB　All the films listed above are distributed by Concord Films,
201 Felixstowe Road, Ipswich, Suffolk, IP3 9BJ.

Books

Crispin Aubery (ed.): *Nukespeak: The Media and the Bomb* ...(Comedia, 1982).,

Bradshaw, Gould and Jones (eds): *From Protest to Resistance* (Mushroom/Peace News, 1981).

John Collins: *Faith Under Fire* (Leslie Frewin, 1966).

John Cox: *Overkill* (Penguin, 3rd edition, 1981).

Christopher Driver: *The Disarmers* (Hodder & Stoughton, 1964).

Peggy Duff: *Left, Left, Left* (Allison & Busby, 1971).

A.J.R. Groom: *British Thinking About Nuclear Weapons* (Frances Pinter, 1974).

F. Parkin: *Middle Class Radicalism* (Manchester University Press, 1968).

R. Taylor and C. Pritchard: *The Protest Makers* (Pergamon, 1980).

Notes on Contributors

FRANK ALLAUN is MP for Salford East. He helped to organise the first Aldermaston march in 1958, and has marched nearly every year since in Britain or West Germany. He was chairman of the Labour Party in 1980, and has remained a member of its National Executive Committee. His many pamphlets include the recent, widely read *Questions and Answers on Nuclear Weapons* written for CND.

PAT ARROWSMITH is an assistant editor at Amnesty International. She was organising secretary for the first Aldermaston march while working for the Direct Action Committee Against Nuclear War (DAC). She has also worked full-time for *Peace News*, and the Committee of 100, and Merseyside CND. By 1983 she had been jailed ten times for her beliefs. She has stood as a candidate in three general elections. Publications include three novels, a play and two collections of poems and pictures, one for CND: *On the Brink*.

CATHY ASHTON works for the Social Work Training Council. She worked full-time for CND, 1977-9, and has since been national treasurer and is now a CND vice-chairperson.

ALASDAIR BEAL is a civil engineer. He joined CND as a student in Glasgow in 1973, has been an active campaigner since then in London, the Potteries and Leeds and has been a member of CND National Council since 1975. At present, in addition to national and local work, he designs and promotes badges for Leeds CND.

PHILIP BOLSOVER is a free-lance journalist and writer. Editor of *Sanity*, 1965-71, he is now chairman of Sanity Editorial board. He has been a member of the National Council since 1971. He is the author of numerous articles and other writings for CND, including *Civil Defence — the Cruellest Confidence Trick*, a CND best-seller and has written children's books and TV scripts as well as publications on political affairs. He is a member of Brighton CND.

JOHN BRUNNER is the author of nearly 100 books, including the award-winning *Stand on Zanzibar* (1968). He has supported CND actively since it began. In 1959 he and his wife, Marjorie, toured seven European countries with the CND exhibition *No Place to Hide*. He is best known in the Campaign for the song "The H-Bombs' Thunder".

JANEY BUCHAN is MEP for Glasgow. She has been involved with CND on the Clydeside from the earliest years, as well as working for the Labour Party and serving for many years as a city councillor. She shares with her husband Norman, a love of folk music and has organised major concerts in Glasgow.

NORMAN BUCHAN is MP for Renfrewshire West and Labour's chief spokesman on agriculture. He has actively supported CND since it began. Elected chairman of the Tribune Group of Labour MPs in 1981. He was described by Pete Seeger in the mid-Sixties as "Britain's first folk MP".

RIP BULKELEY joined CND in 1961. He was chairman of Oxford University branch and a member of the Oxford Committee of 100. He was recently active at several levels from local neighbourhood to Southern Region CND committee, and co-ordinator in the Oxford Campaign Against the Missiles (Campaign ATOM). He is an active supporter of END and has taken part in demonstrations in Brussels, Paris and Bonn. Besides several CND songs, he has written "Making Nuclear Disarmament Happen" and other discussion articles on CND strategy as well as a short history of the movement.

IAN CAMPBELL is best known as leader of the Ian Campbell Folk Group, formed in 1957 and fully professional from 1963 to 1977. The group sang at CND demonstrations and benefits regularly from 1958 and recorded twenty-four LPs with many peace songs, including Ian's "The Sun is Burning". He recently took a degree in Theatre Studies and describes himself as a "freelance writer and unemployed teacher".

APRIL CARTER is a lecturer in politics at Oxford University and a member of the Alternative Defence Commission. She was full time secretary of the Direct Action Committee Against Nuclear War, 1958-61; worked for *Peace News*, 1961-2, and was chairperson of CND, 1970-71. Among other books, she has written *Direct Action and Liberal Democracy*, 1973.

154 THE CND STORY

HOWARD CLARK is a member of the Bradford Nuclear Disarmament Group. He is a researcher at Bradford University School of Peace Studies and worked for the Alternative Defence Commission; was a co-editor of *Peace News*, with which paper he has a long association, and is the author of the recent CND pamphlet *Atoms for War* and the *Peace News* pamphlet *Making non-violent Revolution*.

IAN DAVISON teaches in a Glasgow comprehensive school. He was active in CND during the early 1960s, kept in touch in the late 1960s and became really active again from 1972. Secretary of Scottish CND, 1975-81, he has since become secretary of the Scottish Campaign Against Trident (SCAT) as well as a member of the National Council and the executive of British CND.

ZOE FAIRBAIRNS is a journalist and novelist, author of *Benefits* and *Stand We At Last*, recently published by Virago. She was editor of *Sanity*, 1973-4, and also wrote the CND pamphlet *Study War No More*. She lives in South London and is actively involved in the women's liberation movement.

JOHN FREMLIN joined CND in its first year and marched on four successive years from Aldermaston. He did a considerable amount of public speaking for the Campaign in its active years, and again recently. He was Professor of Applied Radioactivity at the University of Birmingham until 1981. He was scientific consultant to Cumbria County Council in the Windscale Inquiry, and has been closely concerned with the relative risks of different methods of power production.

ROBERT FYSON teaches history at North Staffs Polytechnic. He has been a supporter of CND since 1958, worked as full-time regional organiser for East Anglia CND, 1962-3. Since 1970 he has spent seven years as a Liberal councillor, and has stood twice as Liberal parliamentary candidate in Newcastle-under-Lyme. He has been Secretary of Liberal CND and Peace Group since 1980, and is a member of CND National Council.

RICHARD GOTT is features editor of the *Guardian*. In 1959 he was on the executive committee of the Combined Universities CND; and was later a member of CND's National Council and of the Independent Nuclear Disarmament Election Committee (INDEC). He stood as Radical Alliance candidate in the 1966 Hull North by-election, campaigning primarily against British government support for America's Vietnam war policy.

DAVID GRIFFITHS works for the Labour Party as a research officer. He was editor of *Sanity*, 1974-6, secretary of Labour CND, 1975-8, and its chairperson in 1979-80.

ADRIAN HENRI is a freelance poet-singer-painter-songwriter-lecturer. A supporter of CND and the Committee of 100 throughout the 1960s, he has continued to help the Campaign whenever possible since then. His books include *Autobiography* (1971), *City Hedges* (1977), *From the Loveless Motel* (1980) and *Eric the Punk Cat*, a story for children (1982).

HUGH JENKINS became Lord Jenkins of Putney in 1981. He was chairman of the Mitcham Hydrogen Bomb Campaign Committee in 1954, and was involved with CND from its formation in 1958. More recently, he has been CND's chairperson, 1979-81, and since 1981 vice-president. He was Labour MP for Putney, 1964-79, and Minister for Arts, 1974-6.

MERVYN JONES, novelist and journalist has been active in CND from the time of its foundation. He was chairperson of the Greenwich and Blackheath group, 1958-62, and a regular *Sanity* columnist till the mid-Sixties. Since 1980 he has resumed CND activity, addressing many meetings. His books include *John and Mary*, *Holding On* and *Today the Struggle*, much of which deals with CND's early days.

BRUCE KENT is general secretary of CND. He has been an active member of CND throughout the 1970s and was chairperson, 1977-9. He is a Catholic priest and a former chairperson of War on Want.

ISOBEL LINDSAY teaches sociology at Strathclyde University. She joined CND in 1960, helped organise the 1960s campaign against the Holy Loch Polaris base, and continues to be "a rank-and-file CND member". More recently, she has become Executive vice-chairperson of the Scottish National Party.

RUTH LONGONI is a teacher. She is an active member of Coventry CND, and Trade-Union Liaison Officer for West Midlands Region CND.

JOHN MINNION teaches Complementary Studies at Birmingham Polytechnic. An active supporter of CND since 1959, he worked as full-time regional organiser for West Midlands CND, 1963-65, as full-time fund-raiser for National CND, 1965-66, and as temporary general secretary, 1967. He is a member of Selly Oak CND

ADRIAN MITCHELL is a poet, novelist and playwright. He was a member of the Committee Against the Hydrogen Bomb at Oxford University in 1954, joined CND in 1959 and has supported it ever since. He has written many poems about World War III and read them at CND rallies and on many other occasions in Britain and abroad; most of these are included in his recently published collected poems, 1953-79, *For Beauty Douglas* (1982).

DICK NETTLETON is chairman of Farringdon (Oxon) Peace Group and was formerly general secretary of CND (1967-73). He joined Bolton CND in 1958 and became full-time organiser for North-West Region CND throughout, but thinks the most important thing he ever did was to organise demonstrations in the late 1960s in Birkenhead and Barrow against the launch of each of Britain's four Polaris submarines.

SHEILA OAKES is general secretary of the National Peace Council; She has been a supporter of the Campaign since its earliest years and was national chairperson 1967-8. Since then she has also travelled extensively, representing British peace organisations abroad.

PAUL OESTREICHER is a priest of the Church of England, Canon of Southwark Cathedral and secretary of the International Affairs Division of the British Council of Churches. He has been active in CND almost since it started, was formerly chairman of Amnesty International. He is one of the authors of *The Church and the Bomb*.

ANDREW PAPWORTH has been a social worker since 1972. He joined his first Aldermaston march in 1960, worked as full-time secretary of the London Committee of 100, 1965-6 and was also a National Council member for several years. In 1968 he was deported from Moscow for his part in the War Resisters' International's "Save Czechoslovakia" activities. He is a member of Kilburn CND.

JOHN PETHERBRIDGE is a playwright and scriptwriter. He went on his first Aldermaston march in 1962 and has been a CND supporter ever since. He was a member of the editorial board of CND's paper *Sanity* for some years during the 1970s and has written a wide variety of articles for the paper.

DUNCAN REES is a full-time organiser for CND; he has been active in the Campaign since joining Cardiff Youth CND at the end of the 1960s, and was general secretary of CND, 1976-9. He rejoined the staff in 1981. During the interim he was a vice-chairperson of British CND and chairperson of London Region.

JO RICHARDSON is MP for Barking (London). She has been associated with CND since its formation, was a vice-chairperson 1974-81, and since then has become a vice-president. She is also a member of the National Executive of the Labour Party and an executive member of the National Council for Civil Liberties.

JOAN RUDDOCK became chairperson of CND in 1981 and was re-elected unopposed in 1982. In 1980 she was a co-founder of Newbury Campaign Against Cruise Missiles (CND) and was elected to CND National Council. In the late 1960s the early 1970s she worked for Shelter and subsequently for other helping agencies. She is now on the staff of a Citizens' Advice Bureau and stood as Labour Parliamentary candidate for Newbury in 1979.

TONY SIMPSON teaches at the University of Wales. He joined CND in 1959, took part in the early Aldermaston marches and some Committee of 100 activities. He wrote the recent pamphlet *H-Bomb on Ogwr*, which sets out the effects of a nuclear attack on Wales and *No Bunkers Here*, which describes in detail the direct action at Bridgend. He is a member of Mid-Glamorgan CND.

DAN SMITH is a researcher and writer. He came into CND in the early 1970s. He was general secretary, 1974-5, continued to play an active part as treasurer and is now a National Council member. He is also chairperson of END and a member of the Alternative Defence Commission. Author of *The Defence of the Realm in the 1980s* and co-editor of *Protest and Survive* (1980), and *Disarming Europe* (1982).

VAL STEVENS is an environmental publicist (writer, speaker, broadcaster) and sometime teacher and housewife. She has been a supporter of CND for some years, and in 1981 was elected to West Midlands CND executive committee. She has been a member of the Conservation Society since 1971, of Friends of the Earth since 1974, and in 1979 was a founder member of the Anti-Nuclear Campaign.

EDWARD THOMPSON is a writer and historian. He was active in CND during the late 1950s and in the 1960s. He wrote the pamphlet *Protest and Survive* in response to the civil defence booklet *Protect and Survive* and the government's nuclear policies which it reflected. His other publications include *The Making of the English Working Class* (1963), *Beyond the Cold War* (1981) and *Zero Option* (1982).

ALISON WHYTE works for CND as press and publicity officer. She joined the staff in 1981, having previously been with Friends of the Earth. Before this she was a teacher active in the women's liberation movement.

WALTER WOLFGANG is an accountant. One of the four-person committee formed to organise the first Aldermaston march, he has been active in CND during the entire twenty-five years since then; for most of that period he has been a National Council member. He is Vice-chairperson of Labour CND and a committee member of London Region CND. He is active in the Labour Party, and a former parliamentary candidate.

PETER WORSLEY has been Professor of Sociology at Manchester University since 1964. He was a member of the New Left of the late 1950s and has supported CND since its formation. He was a member of the National Council until the late 1960s and has returned to more active involvement in the 1980s. His books include, as editor, the standard sociology textbook, *Introducing Sociology* (Penguin).

NIGEL YOUNG is Reader in Peace Studies at Bradford University. He has been in CND since it was founded; became full-time regional organiser for London CND 1961-2 and for West Midlands CND during the following year. He is currently involved in developing transnational peace education, and is active in END. He has published a book on the New Left, *An Infantile Disorder?* (1977); his main book *War Resistance and the Nation State* is currently in production, and he is at present writing one on disarmament strategy.

Other books of interest from Allison & Busby

Michael Bagley
THE PLUTONIUM FACTOR
Michael Bagley's fast-paced, highly realistic thriller shows how a determined terrorist gang could hijack used plutonium rods from a civilian nuclear reactor and use them to fashion a primitive but deadly bomb.

Mordecai Roshwald
LEVEL 7
The most powerful anti-nuclear novel yet to be written. "A masterpiece about the holocaust and its aftermath ... It is wholly compelling and, quite simply, a classic" *New Statesman*.

Adrian Mitchell
FOR BEAUTY DOUGLAS
Collected Poems 1953-1979
Illustrated throughout by Ralph Steadman
"Mitchell is a joker, a lyrics writer, a word-spinner, an epigrammist, a man of passion and imagination" *John Berger*. "We're lucky to have Adrian in the platoon. Out there in the dark, firing away. Urging us on. And then coming home into the light to make us laugh" *Roger McGough*.

Hilary Wainwright and Dave Elliott
THE LUCAS PLAN
A New Trade Unionism in the Making?
The first full account of the worker's campaign at Lucas Aerospace to defend their jobs and the plan to convert the company's resources from defence production to the development of socially useful products. "Seldom in recent industrial history can there have been such an imaginative and, at the same time, practical response to the problems of unemployment and industrial decline" *Tribune*.

Anthony Barnett
IRON BRITANNIA
Why Parliament Waged Its Falklands War
Anthony Barnett's witty sardonic and factual account answers the question: why did the war happen at all? And he argues that the unleashed passions of national pride exhibited by British Leaders of all parties, seem to confirm the pessimistic warnings of those who presage a nuclear holocaust. "One of the liveliest pieces of expert polemic this country has seen for many years" *John Fowles*.

Stephen Bodington
SCIENCE AND SOCIAL ACTION
With an introduction by Mike Cooley
"Will science destroy us? Can science save us?" In a book designed for the non-specialist reader, Stephen Bodington tackles some of the problems posed by these contradictory but inseparable questions. "Triply welcome" *Time Out*. "Fundamental and wide-ranging" Ian Mikado, *Labour Weekly*.

Alan Roberts
THE SELF-MANAGING ENVIRONMENT
A far-reaching assessment of environmental dilemmas in their social context; it is neither a treatise on Doomsday nor an apologia for unrestricted and unpredictable "advance".

All these books are available from good bookshops, or can be ordered direct from the CND Bookshop, 227 Seven Sisters Road, London N4.

ORDER FORM

...The Plutonium Factor	Michael Bagley	£7.95
...Level 7	Mordecai Roshwald	£1.95
...For Beauty Douglas	Adrian Mitchell	£4.95
...The Lucas Plan	Hilary Wainwright & Dave Elliott	£2.95
...Iron Britannia	Anthony Barnett	£2.95
...Science and Social Action	Stephen Bodington	£3.50
...The Self-Managing Environment	Alan Roberts	£3.95

NAME ....

ADDRESS ....

....

Send to the CND Bookshop, 227 Seven Sisters Road, London N4.

Please enclose remittance to the value of the cover price plus: 30p for the first book plus 15p for each additional book ordered to a maximum charge of £1.05 to cover postage and packing. Applicable only in the UK.

While every effort is made to keep prices low, it is sometimes necessary to increase prices at short notice. Allison & Busby reserve the right to show on covers and charge new retail prices which may differ from those advertised in the text or elsewhere.